LIVE LIFE

A Spiritual Guide To Declaring Freedom
In Every Area Of Your Life

DANA MARIE

Copyright © 2018 Dana Marie

Live Life Free: A Spiritual Guide To Declaring Freedom In Every Area Of Your Life

ISBN-13: 978-0-9998378-0-1

All rights reserved. No part of this publication may be reproduced, distributed, or transmitted in any form or by any means, including photocopying, recording, or other electronic or mechanical methods, or by any information storage and retrieval system without the prior written permission of the publisher, except, in the case of very brief quotations embodied in critical review and certain other noncommercial uses permitted by copyright law.

1 2 3 4 5 6 7 8 9 10

Edit & Layout by: Good Ground Literary Services, LLC
Book Cover Design: ABenson Media
Photography: TanyaR Photography

ACKNOWLEDGEMENTS

Firstly, I'd like to give honor and thanks to God for entrusting me with the vision of this book and allowing it to come to fruition. Next, I'd like to thank my lovely fiancé, Warren, for his continuous support, prayers, and encouragement throughout my journey. I'd like to thank my amazing daughter, Jaisa, for being my "WHY" and holding me accountable for executing God's plan for our family. I'd also like to thank my mother, Darlene Randolph, for instilling Godly principles in me as well as teaching me how to forgive, let go and let God. Lastly, a special thanks to Andre Benson, Davita Garfield, Sharai Robbin, Nateshia Wanamaker, the Good Ground Literary Services team and all my friends and family who supported me in the process. Without you all I know I wouldn't have come this far. Thank you from the bottom of my heart!

TABLE OF CONTENTS

Introduction: Captive! xi

Part One:
Spiritual Freedom

Chapter One: CHRISTIAN BY DEFAULT 3
Chapter Two: Confident Christianity..13
Chapter Three: Believing His Promises...21

Part Two:
Mental Freedom

Chapter Four: Tainted, But Still Forgave..31
Chapter Five: Stop The Stigma. Go Get Help! 39
Chapter Six: Renew Your Thoughts: Positivity Only!......................49

Part Three:
Relationship Freedom

Chapter Seven: The Usual Family Drama 61
Chapter Eight: Friends Or "Frenemies" 69
Chapter Nine: Agape Love...77

Part Four:
Financial Freedom

Chapter Ten: Budgeting: The Master Plan..89
Chapter Eleven: The Life Saver 97
Chapter Twelve: Slaves To The Lender..105

Part Five:
Career Freedom

Chapter Thirteen: Do What You Love 115
Chapter Fourteen: Walking In Your Purpose 123
Chapter Fifteen: Boss Living = Boss Sacrifice 131

Part Six:
The Final Declaration

ChapterSixteen: #NoLongerBound 141
The Vow 143
References 147
Notes 149

LIVE LIFE

Free

INTRODUCTION

CAPTIVE!

America is known as the land of the free, however, given all that we're facing as a country today, I find that hard to believe. Are we actually the land of the free if we're not permitted to live the life we're "entitled"? We're the American Dream, but every day we're struggling to pay our bills, suffering from depression, and dreading to go to work. Our current president, Donald Trump, has several allegations of sexual assault, yet he remains in office while our society ignores the injustice these women experienced. A society like this, one that ignores the needs of its citizens has affected my life spiritually, mentally, and financially. The government offers assistance like housing allowances and food vouchers to those below poverty guidelines and there are tax breaks for the wealthy elite class, but the middle class continues to live paycheck to paycheck, barely being able to provide food and shelter for their families. I've come to realize that we are not as free as we think we are. We live in the land of the free, but don't have freedom. When I finally opened my Bible, I learned that everything I needed to declare freedom in all areas of my life was right there.

When you are determined enough to take control of your own life, you are finally living in freedom. To be free means you have the power to determine your own fate no matter what obstacles you're faced with while doing so. If you put the word free into the context of your life, free means that you are no longer bound by the fear of walking while being black. You aren't worried about the bills you can't afford to pay because there's no assistance for you as a middle-class worker. You no longer feel inadequate when you get rejected by the people who are supposed to love you. Freedom is exercising control in every area of your life. You may not believe it just yet, but the fact of the matter is you deserve to live life free. This means that you should be experiencing an abundant life without fear, worry or anxiety. You are destined to live a purposeful, prosperous and courageous life filled with love, peace, joy, and freedom. You are destined to live life and live it abundantly!

As a Christian millennial, I believe the best way to gain full control over your life is to surrender your life to Jesus Christ. Allow him to enter in and guide you on the destined path of prosperity *He* created for you long before you were born.

Pause. Okay, I get it. It's confusing. I know you're wondering, "How am I in full control of my life if Jesus is in full control of my life?"

I'm glad you asked. The bible says, "For to me, to live is Christ and to die is gain (Philippians 1:21)," which means that you are giving up your life to follow Jesus, live as he lived, and have a prosperous life. I'm sure you think you know what's best for you, but God knows more about you than you will ever know.

> *"No eye has seen, no ear has heard, and no mind has imagined what God has prepared for those who love him."*
> 1 Corinthians 2:9

God knows the exact hour you will receive your financial breakthrough. He knows the exact minute you'll find your soul mate. He knows everything you'll endure, good and bad, but you must trust him enough to lead you because he knows best. (See Proverbs 3:5-6)

"You take full control over your life when you give Jesus Christ full control over your life."

For a long time, I was trying to live life without seeking God's counsel. I was pivoting downhill because my faith was too weak to trust in God's plan, so I made my own decisions. I decided to stay in bad, abusive relationships. I decided to keep quiet about the pain I was experiencing in my youth from sexual assault. I also decided to fault God for everything that happened. What I didn't realize is that all I had to do was ask God to lead me on the right path and he would have.

> *"If any of you lacks wisdom, you should ask God,*
> *who gives generously to all without finding fault,*
> *and it will be given to you."*
> James 1:5

Instead, I decided to make my own choices, resulting in pain and setbacks that God truly never intended to happen to me.

In this book, you'll learn about my real-life, personal experiences with the bondage of financial hardships and abusive relationships among other things, as well as, how I escaped and began living a life full of freedom. I can truly say that it was, and still is, by the grace of God that I'm alive to share my story with you. I was captive in every area of my life; controlled by the false hopes of American culture and succumbing to the harsh realities of my surroundings. Even more, I was spiritually confused. I didn't know if I should trust God or believe the lies the devil had planted inside my head. Most of my relationships, intimate and platonic, were imbalanced. I was mostly always the giver and my friends and family were typically the takers. My finances were all over the place, the debt was piling up and I couldn't afford to take care of my bills. I was struggling with finding a career that made me happy. My mind was racing all the time with worries about life. But, thanks to the word of God I found and utilized biblical principles that served as an escape plan to my freedom.

If you are not a believer in Christ, then this book may not be for you. I can only tell you what I know, and I know for sure that from the moment I surrendered my life to Christ and began to follow his will, I began to live life free.

Let me inform you that what you're about to read has "no filter." It's raw and uncut. I want you to experience the utmost authentic me, mainly because I'm almost 100% sure you will see part of yourself. For me to obtain freedom I had to first become transparent with myself. I took a look in the mirror, at the real me, and not the person I portrayed to others. To others, I was well-kept and successful, charismatic, and optimistic. Once I started to truly examine myself, I realized that there was a disconnect between who I was and who I appeared to be. To myself, I was worthless and flawed. I'd smile in your face, but deep down inside the river Jordan was flowing from the countless tears. I'd let people borrow my last $100, when I didn't even have enough money to pay my own rent. I'd stand in a room full of people, exuding confidence, but in all actuality, I was whimpering like a sixth grader introducing herself to her new class. I was miserable, depressed and lonely, but I hid it all inside. To the world, I was strong, happy and funny and no one could tell that inside I was suffering. I dealt with depression, molestation, and financial turmoil, just to name a few, but no one ever knew that I was struggling to live life. I should have won an Oscar for my performances, however, the pretending became overwhelming, so I decided it was time to take off the chains, remove the mask and uncover the skeletons. Honestly, going after my freedom was one of the best decision I've made thus far.

"Be sure the person you see in the mirror is actually you."

My first inkling was to run to God because I know He is faithful and his mercies endure forever. I knew God would forgive me and show me how to get out of the mess I was in. As I began to pray and indulge more in God's word I realized that I was one of many Christians who failed to use the bible as a blueprint for their life. I recognized that in order for me to become free I had to first understand what types of bondage I was in, and then create the necessary escape route to freedom using God's word.

As you read this book you will realize that you and I were in some of the same prisons. Let me name a few, "Fear and Discouragement Penitentiary." Throughout writing this book, I was so scared to step out on faith that I missed every deadline I set. I didn't want to be judged for my past, so I gave up writing a few times. Then there's "Broke and Always in Debt Prison." I couldn't get my hair or nails done because I had so much debt and so many other financial responsibilities that treating myself caused stress and more credit card charges, so crusty feet it was. There's also "Depression and Self-Doubt Asylum." I was tormented by the negative thoughts, *"You're worthless. You're a disgrace. You'll never amount to anything."* I was in a mental nut house and I was the only lonely patient.

Just as it was for me, it's the captivity of your mind that's preventing you from living life free – from starting your business, writing your book or even beginning your family. God warns us that our fight is far more than earthly matters, it's mental and spiritual.

> *"For our struggle is not against flesh and blood, but against the rulers, against the authorities, against the powers of this dark world and against the spiritual forces of evil in the heavenly realms."*
> Ephesians 6:12

Those spiritual and internal prisons are making you okay with being just okay! You're content with the lies the devil tells you and the strongholds he has in your life. But, I came here to tell you that God has equipped you with the tools to win the war for your freedom. He said put on the belt of truth, the breastplate of righteousness, the helmet of salvation, feet shod with the gospel of peace, the shield of faith, and the sword of the spirit, all which will help you win the good fight. You are more than ordinary. You are amazingly extraordinary. That's why the Devil has to try so hard to destroy you. You were made to be *GREAT* and live *ABUNDANTLY*!

> *"The thief comes only to steal and kill and destroy; I have come that they may have life, and have it to the full."*
> John 10:10

Although you are in captivity right now, your escape is underway. This book will guide you through the process of living life free in five major areas of your life: your spiritual, mental, and financial life, as well as your relationships and career. Each section is broken down into three chapters, which also include eight biblically supported tips that I personally used on my journey to freedom. Through extensive bible study, I realized that the word of God gives us everything we need to escape the bondage and live life free. Why not utilize it?

> *"All Scripture is God-breathed and is useful for teaching, rebuking, correcting and training in righteousness, so that the servant of God may be thoroughly equipped for every good work."*
> 2 Timothy 3:16-17

Now listen, I'm giving you the tools necessary to escape to freedom. What you do with it is up to you. I don't expect you to read this book passively. I want you to get involved in the freedom process. Get your bible out or download the Bible app on your phone because you'll want to highlight and mark up the scriptures that will help you during this journey. Get ready to do some digging under the surface to find out what's holding you captive and then, by any means necessary, break out of that prison. Are you ready to be a fugitive and live life free? If so, your great escape begins now!

SPIRITUAL FREEDOM

CHAPTER ONE

CHRISTIAN BY DEFAULT

It's Sunday morning; the house is filled with a sweet aroma. You can smell the turkey wings baking in the oven, the sweet potatoes candying on the stove, and the collard greens simmering on the burner. My mother would yell up the steps to her nine children, the ones she birthed plus the ones she took in, "Wake up. It's time for church!"

We'd all wake up simultaneously to get washed and dressed in our best church clothes, making sure we were fashionable and appeared suitable for the people of God. Luckily, our church was less than two blocks away from our house, so we didn't have to rush. We went to an old church in a worn beige building with burgundy cushioned pews and tall pillars in the front of the sanctuary. Even though our church always seemed to be under construction, there was a huge mirrored pulpit that sat out like a main stage for some grand performance.

Once inside, my siblings and I spread out to fill the pews between our church friends. We'd dare not talk or play around because someone was bound to whisper about how my mother's children had no home training. We did not want to feel her wrath, so we'd sit quietly, occasionally giggling at the moans and groans of the holy saints as they basked in the presence of God.

For the most part, I was too young, and perhaps too spiritually immature, to understand speaking in tongues. And since I didn't really understand the messages being delivered, I rarely listened to what was being said. I never processed the meaning of being a Christian until one day one of the church mothers asked me if I was saved and had I accepted Jesus Christ as my personal savior.

I froze like an iceberg, too stiff and stubborn to respond. Firstly, I was trying to figure out why she asked me out of the twenty plus youth in the church. Then, I was too prideful to ask her to explain what she meant because I was a "Miss Know-It-All."

As she stared into my eyes waiting for my answer, I took a deep gulp of my pride and said, "Yes."

"How do you know?" she replied.

I took a second gulp and said, "I'm saved because I go to church."

Chuckling, she said, "Dana, the church doesn't save you. Jesus does." Then she walked away shaking her head as if I was a disgrace to her and the church.

I was only eight years old and I didn't understand what she meant. I never paid attention to the sermons or alter calls enough to know what being saved was. I thought I was saved because my mother made me go to church, encouraged me to sing in the choir, and dance on the praise team. I was doing the right things, so I thought all was well. After church, I went to one of the Sunday school teachers to question her about what it meant to be saved. She sat me in the tiny Lil Tikes chair to explained that being saved meant I had to develop a personal relationship with Jesus Christ, admitted and accepted that *He* is the Son of God who was crucified, buried and raised from the dead for my sins.

I didn't know it then, but me thinking that going to church meant I was saved made me a Christian by default. I didn't know Jesus personally. Since my mother went to church and her mother went to church the belief was passed down from generation to generation without a clear explanation of what being a Christian meant. I believe this is still one of the biggest mistakes Christians make today. So many people say they are Christians because they go to church, they serve in ministry, they follow the tradition and some even pay their tithes. But so few Christians *really* know Jesus. What I found is that the first step to initiating the process of spiritual freedom is to accept the Lord and Savior, the God of Truth, the Father of Love, Jesus Christ as *your* personal savior. This means to develop a relationship with him and to live like him. The reason God sent his son was to show us how to live, work and enjoy life; the good the bad and the ugly. To get to freedom live a life like Jesus. Jesus is the way, the truth, and the light, and he will set you free.

> *"Then you will know the truth,*
> *and the truth will set you free."*
> John 8:32

Once I accepted the Lord as my personal savior I thought that I'd be free from all my troubles. Although it took me another two years to finally get "saved," I was sure God was pleased with my decision and that life was going to be a breeze from this point on. I was on fire for Jesus and no one and nothing could stop me. For the first time in my life, at twelve years old, I experienced the power of the Holy Spirit. I was in my mom's room listening to praise and worship music with my hands lifted high and tears rolling down my face as I proudly proclaimed the name and power of the almighty God. Suddenly this overwhelming presence filled the air and even when my older brother walked in on me, laughing and teasing me for "catching the holy ghost", I didn't stop worshipping. The more he laughed, the louder I worshipped and the harder I clapped. The power of the Holy Spirit filled the room so much that my brother fled like the devil when we resist him and submit to God. (See James 4:7)

After my impartation of the Holy Spirit, I naturally assumed that all Christians were going to act like the fruits of the spirit they talk about in the bible. I believed everyone who went to church was loving, caring, humble, kind and gentle. I knew for sure church folk wouldn't treat me like my brother did, laughing and scolding me for praising God and trying to live a righteous life. However, that wasn't the case. I experienced a lot of hurt from the people who were supposed to be Christ-like. This pain came from the same people who were preaching and teaching the word of God, hosting hour-long Sunday school, Tuesday evening bible study and all night 24 hour /7 days a week prayer. Can you say disappointed?

Every week I had to memorize a new bible verse for Sunday School. I was in church praying more than I played outside. I served as a pastor's aid and choir member because I wanted to prove to God that I was devoted to being his vessel. I made huge sacrifices that most kids won't willingly make to serve God. Freeze tag outside with friends or choir practice. Choir practice! Sunday birthday parties at Chuck E Cheese or church all day. Church all day! Those are big decisions for a kid. Deep down in my soul, I desired to be more Christ-like, but I still wanted to be a kid. So, I tried to bridge the gap between having a fun childhood and being a devoted Christian. I discussed fun kid-friendly ways to teach the word of God and recommended contemporary gospel songs to worship to. I wanted the church to be fun and not have to feel like a prison for kids so that the choice to follow Jesus could be much easier. For whatever reason, the church wasn't too receptive to my ideas. They were actually angry with me for trying to bridge this gap. I was scolded for dancing to "secular" gospel music as if my soul intention wasn't to glorify God. I was criticized for sharing ways to make Sunday school fun. I was judged for not being as spiritually mature as I should have been according to their standards. I kept wondering, "How could these people who shoved Christ down your throat for breakfast, lunch, and dinner be so unappreciative of my efforts to serve God?"

My only conclusion was that they too, were Christian by default, caught up in the religion and not the relationship with Christ. I realized that these same people were human beings living in the flesh and were susceptible to making mistakes. In the flesh, these people were judgmental, harsh, mean and unempathetic, but as believers, it's our job to crucify our flesh daily and die to self. If they had focused more on establishing and growing in their relationship with Christ as well as living life like him then they would have shown more of the fruits of the spirit. Jesus was crucified, put to death and nailed to a cross, to take away all our sins. When you nail yourself and your sin to the cross (crucify your flesh) you no longer live for you, you live for Christ. Your actions, your attitude, your behaviors should resemble Jesus because you have now transitioned from being a Christian by default to personally knowing God for yourself. You will live the life God intended you to live because he ultimately knows best.

For to me, to live is Christ and to die is gain.
Philippians 1:21

The road to spiritual freedom begins with first acknowledging that you may not be in a relationship with Jesus Christ. I realized it at eight years old. I was just going with the flow of church, doing what I was told to do. Standing when it was time to stand, reading when it was time to read and giving when it was time to give. The true connection was missing. So, I ask, are you truly saved or are you just Christian by default? Next, understand that everyone in this world is human; we will all make mistakes and fall short of the glory of God. And did you know that the deacons and ministers at your church, my church, his church, and her church are human too? They might be mean to you, they might judge you and they might hate on you because they too fall short.

> *"For all have sinned and fall short of the glory of God, and all are justified freely by his grace through the redemption that came by Christ Jesus."*
> Romans 3:23-24

Lastly, to my fellow Christians, you must strengthen and grow *your* personal relationship with Jesus Christ, so that his qualities can rub off on you. Stop listening to the religious talk about who Christ is and get to know him for yourself. It's one thing to know about him, but when you actually know him, the relationship will be greater than anything you could imagine. He's waiting for you to seek for him. He's waiting for you to open your heart and accept him. He wants an intimate relationship with you. The question is, do you?

If you want to, here are eights tips to help build and establish an intimate relationship with God.

Dana Marie's 8 Tips for a Real Relationship with Christ

- **Choose to follow Jesus.**

First, accept the Lord and Savior, the God of Truth, the Father of Love, Jesus Christ as your personal savior by admitting that he is the Son of God, who came to save us from sin. Acknowledge that he was crucified, buried and rose three days later with all power in his hands. The only way to be a true Christian is to confess, believe and conform.

> *"If you declare with your mouth, "Jesus is Lord," and believe in your heart that God raised him from the dead, you will be saved."*
> Romans 10:9

- **Talk to God every day; PRAY.**

The bible teaches us to pray without ceasing which means talk to him non-stop. Think of Jesus as your best friend. You can let him know how you feel even when you're upset. Talk about your day. Ask those simple questions you think you already know the answer to. Share your greatest desires with God. He listens, and he cares, just like a good friend will!

> *"I no longer call you servants, because a servant does not know his master's business. Instead, I have called you friends, for everything that I learned from my Father I have made known to you."*
> John 15:15

- **Read and study the bible.**

You can study the character of Jesus, his teachings and how he lived his life by reading the word. Reading the Bible helps you to navigate through life's test, both good and bad. You can read about how even Jesus was tempted. The devil promised him the entire kingdom of the Earth. For us now, that would mean money, cars, all life's luxuries and more, but Jesus said no because he knew he had a greater purpose than to serve the devil. Can you be like Jesus and turn down wealth and riches to follow your purpose? You can look at the Bible as your blueprint for life. For every situation you're facing today, God has already given you the answer on how to make it through in his word.

> *"Keep this Book of the Law always on your lips;*
> *meditate on it day and night, so that you may*
> *be careful to do everything written in it.*
> *Then you will be prosperous and successful."*
> Joshua 1:8

- **Make the daily choice to crucify your flesh.**
You will need to make daily sacrifices that will bring you closer to Christ and the plan he has for you. God wants to see that you are willing to give up your own fleshy desires such as sexual sin, gossiping or even gluttony to live a life as Christ did. Every day you have an opportunity to stop cursing so much and to not send out that "booty call" text, but you must make a conscious decision to sacrifice your fleshly desires for the desires of Christ.

> *"Then he said to the crowd, "If any of you wants*
> *to be my follower, you must turn from your selfish ways,*
> *take up your cross daily and follow me."*
> Luke 9:23 NLT

- **Embody the essence of Jesus.**

As your love for Jesus grows you will become so intertwined with him that you begin to act like him, to embody his character. Before you act on any situation, ask yourself, What Would Jesus Do? Would he curse out that irritating co-worker? No, he wouldn't. He would be kind and loving towards them.

Sometimes, we forget that we aren't living as us anymore, we are living as Christ. You and Christ should become one so much so that everything you do is the same. You should act like him, talk like him, respond like him, lead like him, forgive like him, love like him, party like him and serve like him.

> *"Whoever claims to live in him must live as Jesus did"*
> 1 John 2:6

- **Avoid putting yourself in tempting situations.**

The flesh is weak. Try to avoid people and places that trigger your old habits and sinful nature. Sometimes your flesh can take full control over you, especially if you're spending time in unhealthy places. If you were recently delivered from drugs, don't go to the crack house. Struggling with adultery, don't allow you and the opposite sex to be alone at any time. Although you have the power of God in you, you are still human. Avoid anything that could lead you back down sin's path.

> *"So, if you think you are standing firm, be careful that you don't fall! No temptation has overtaken you except what is common to mankind"*
> 1 Corinthians 10:12-13

- **Understand that you can have fun while following Jesus.**

You don't have to stop celebrating with friends, going out to the movies or listening to your favorite love songs just because you're a believer now. It's perfectly okay to have a fun, fulfilling life and still be a believer. Jesus had fun, he partied, tastefully, and was genuinely happy. You can have a glass of wine, just don't get drunk. You can have sex, just make sure it's with your spouse. God truly intended for us to have an enjoyable life.

> *"So I recommend having fun, because there is nothing better for people in this world than to eat, drink, and enjoy life. That way they will experience some happiness along with all the hard work God gives them under the sun."*
> Ecclesiastes 8:15 NLT

- **Be grateful for how far you've come.**

Continue to have moments with God where you acknowledge and thank him for bringing you out of the darkness and into the light. Reminisce about your life before God. Look at how far you've come. Mean and arrogant to humble and understanding. Selfish and stingy to sacrificial and giving. God brought you a long way and he will continue to do so if you stay steadfast on the journey of continuously changing for the betterment of the body of Christ.

> *"And now, just as you accepted Christ Jesus as your Lord, you must continue to follow him. Let your roots grow down into him, and let your lives be built on him. Then your faith will grow strong in the truth you were taught, and you will overflow with thankfulness."*
> Colossians 2:6-7 NLT

As you go from being Christian by default to forming a real relationship with Christ, take into consideration that Jesus served his people, prayed, fasted, studied, and lived a righteous life. Our desire is to be like him - free from the captivities of this world and living in perfect peace.

Although Jesus's spirit was in perfect peace, his life was just like ours. God came to earth in human form as Jesus to show us how he wanted us to live life. He experienced temptation, hurt, and anger, but he also experienced love, fun and joy. Jesus stayed faithful to God and God faithful to him. As a believer, you must remain faithful as Jesus did and remember that the continual process of learning about God is what gives you spiritual freedom. The closer your relationship with God the more you will begin to walk into the destiny he created for you. The more you understand God's word, God's goodness, and God's faithfulness, you will see that he has your best interest at heart. Continue to stay connected to God and get to know him for yourself more and more everyday.

CHAPTER TWO

CONFIDENT CHRISTIANITY

When I look back over my life and all the pain I've experienced, most of it was from so-called Christians. I remember trying to dance with the youth praise team but was rejected without any legitimate reason why. I remember being told I was "fast", and that my outfit was too short for church, even though my skirt hung down slightly below my knees. I remember hearing that I was a "hot mess" because I knew all the boys in the neighborhood and didn't associate with too many girls. I remember being told I wasn't "good enough" to be a leading role in the church play. I remember sharing an amazing idea with the youth leader only to be ridiculed for its stupidity, but then to later find out that they are using my idea. I was devastated and my feelings were completely ignored by the youth leaders and deacons at the church. I was spiritually broken because of these so-called Christians.

    I couldn't wrap my mind around the fact that I had just personally accepted Christ, but the people who served him were hurting me so badly. I remember having a harmless conversation with the church drummer after service when one of the nosey, judgmental deacons told my older sister I was being fast. Without getting my side of the story, my sister hit me in the mouth faster than the speed of light in front of a crowd of people. I didn't even have a chance to redeem myself to my sister, or the deacon who told me, I had no intention of doing anything other than talking. According to the deacon, however, I was trying to make a baby with this guy. I can promise you that that was not what I intended to do.

I was mentally battered by church people and I began to believe every lie they told. I thought I was worthless because my ideas weren't good enough. I felt like I wasn't talented because I couldn't land a major role in any of the church plays. I felt weak because I was always getting hurt by their words. I was a teenager dealing with teenage stuff like acne and fitting in with my peers. I didn't have the time or energy to deal with this mental anguish. Everything I thought and talked about was criticized by the people closest to me. I was completely stressed out. So, I started to read the word of God more and pray harder. I came across a scripture in Matthew 7:15, *"Watch out for false prophets. They come to you in sheep's clothing, but inwardly they are ferocious wolves."*

I had to understand that just because people go to church doesn't mean they know God and live righteously.

I remember being in my mom's room kneeling by her bed, slain in the Holy Spirit while listening to "I Almost Let Go" By Kurt Carr as tears were dripping down my cheeks. The screams arose from deep within the buried pain as I battled for my sounds to be louder than the blasting music. I wanted someone, anyone to hear me, but no human was there, just the spirit of God. In that moment, in the midst of my screams clashing with the rhythm of the music, I heard a thundering voice say, *"Dana, I am here. I am with you. Don't be afraid, my child. Weep not, I am here."*

Then it hit me. I used the back of my hand to erase every tear lingering on my swollen, red face. I stood up tall and said, "I trust you, Father!"

I remembered instantly that I served a mighty God who said I am more than a conqueror. I began to study the word of God specifically searching for the scriptures that validated who I was in Christ. Because I was swimming in the lies that the devil and church people told me, I needed to remind myself of who I was to the everlasting God, as well as tap into the power and authority I was given through him. I was spiritually esteemed, and my confidence in God was increasing because of my diligence in searching for my answers in him.

When you're looking for spiritual freedom, you must have a certain level of confidence. Your confidence in Christ is acquired by knowing who you are in Christ, trusting in his word and believing you are who he said you are, no matter what other people say. Boldly ask God to reveal your worth, because the more you feel worthy, the more confidence you will have. This confidence will allow you to combat every lie and every thought that makes you feel lesser than you truly are. If you're begging the question who am I, I'm glad you asked.

The first step in gaining confidence as a Christian is remembering *whose* you are. Here are eight tips to help boost your confidence and affirm your worth in Christ.

Dana Marie's 8 Tips for Crafting Confident Christians

- **Accept that you are forgiven!**

Say it with me, "I am FORGIVEN!"

No matter what you've done in the past, God most graciously forgives you for it all. If you sincerely ask him to forgive and make a conscious effort to try as hard as you can to flee from temptation, God will continue to give you grace and mercy. No sin is too great to be forgiven.

> *"The Lord our God is merciful and forgiving, even though we have rebelled against him."*
> Daniel 9:9

- **Release your guilty conscious.**

Once you're forgiven God erases all your guilt. Stop holding on to what you've done in the past. It doesn't matter if you stole that money, gave up on your prodigal child, or cursed out the church deacon; you are forgiven and the guilt should be no more. God didn't intend for you to keep those sins in your mind, in fact, God throws your sins into the sea. As big as the sea is, ain't no coming back from that. Let go and let God!

> *"You will again have compassion on us; you will tread our sins underfoot and hurl all our iniquities into the depths of the sea."*
> Micah 7:19

- **Keep your focus on the future.**

Stay away from people who make efforts to remind you of your past and try to use it against you. It's always one or two people that love to bring up your promiscuous ways or gambling problem. Stop listening to those people. Trust me when I tell you, you don't need them in your life. Reconnect with God so he can reassure you of your deliverance and his plan for you.

> *"No, dear brothers and sisters, I have not achieved it, but I focus on this one thing: Forgetting the past and looking forward to what lies ahead, I press on to reach the end of the race and receive the heavenly prize for which God, through Christ Jesus, is calling us."*
> Philippians 3:13 NLT

- **Know that you are valuable.**

God specially handcrafted you to be exactly who you are. Your value is far greater than rubies and diamonds because God is your creator. If Beyoncé and I both tried to sell a pair of our old shoes I might get $3, but she'd probably get $30, 000. Her being the owner places greater value on the shoes. God as your creator makes you more valuable than anything in the world. You were specifically designed to be perfectly you and you are so valuable to God.

> *"I praise you because I am fearfully and wonderfully made; your works are wonderful, I know that full well."*
> Psalms 139:14

- **Realize you are worth it.**

Despite your past mistake and current struggles. With God as your creator, your value is priceless. No one can take that away from you. When the enemy says that you're worthless you say, "WHERE?" Tell the devil you are worth more than he will ever be. Tell your enemies that you are worth it because God said it. Let them know you are forgiven and living. Don't believe the appraisal of men when God already appraised you! Know your worth, believe your worth and exude your worth!

> *"Since you are precious and honored in my sight,*
> *and because I love you, I will give people in exchange*
> *for you, nations in exchange for your life."*
> Isaiah 43:4

- **Live your life full of purpose like God intended.**

Your haters will try to persuade you to believe you have no purpose, no gifts, no talents and no abilities. Your enemies will try to feed you with the fear of success and make you believe your life is meant to be ordinary. I need you to understand that God has major plans for you. When God knitted you together in your mother's womb he knew all the gifts and talents you'd have; he knew the ultimate plan for your life.

> *"For we are God's masterpiece. He has created*
> *us anew in Christ Jesus, so we can do the*
> *good things he planned for us long ago."*
> Ephesians 2:10 NLT

- **Recognize that you are fearless.**

God hasn't given you the spirit of fear. You must tackle every obstacle in your life with confidence. God is with you every step of the way, waiting for you to ask him for support and to pick you up when you fall. Don't fear your enemies. Don't fear the promotion you're not qualified for. Don't settle for anything less than the things God wants you to have – joy, success, peace, love and wisdom.

> *"For God has not given us a spirit of fear,*
> *but of power and of love and of a sound mind."*
> 2 Timothy 1:7 NKJV

- **Understand that you are chosen.**

    Stop allowing people to minimize your abilities because they can't figure out how to do what you do. God chose you, you were appointed to go into the world as a shining star bringing forth light to this dark and ruthless world. Everything that you do, whether speaking, preaching, teaching, or even cooking, serving, sewing, writing, whatever it is it's directly related to the greater purpose God has for your life.

    > *"For you are a holy people, who belong to the Lord your God. Of all the people on earth, the Lord your God has chosen you to be his own special treasure."*
    > Deuteronomy 7:6 NLT

Your spiritual freedom is activated through the understanding of who you are in Christ. Wake up daily with the confidence to defeat every attack the enemy has for your life. Be bold in Christ for you have every right to be. Spend time getting to know God through his word and you will become more spiritually in tune and more confident in who and whose you are.

CHAPTER THREE

BELIEVING HIS PROMISES

When your spiritual life is under attack, the best thing to do is stand on the promises of God. In the Bible, there are several promises that God makes his people. For some reason, although we know these promises, like the songs on the radio, we don't believe them. God says in his word that he will never leave you nor forsake you, so why do you feel alone? God says that he will make your enemies your footstool, so why are you always trying to create a master plan to seek revenge? God says that if you ask for anything in his name he will give it to you, so why are you worrying about your electric bill? God will supply all your needs! God loves you unconditionally and provides you with his magnificent grace. Grace is when God gives you the things you don't deserve, like the new house with a bad credit score. The word of God says, *"my grace is sufficient for thee,"* which indicates that he blesses you with the things that you didn't earn because he loves you. (See 2 Corinthians 12:9)

I'm sure at least once in your life you've overlooked a blessing God gave you, both tangible and intangible. When you fail to realize what the Lord has already done for you, and is continuously doing for you, doubts begin to form about the promises of God. Just because you didn't get the promotion you wanted when you wanted it doesn't mean that God isn't blessing you. Did you forget that you didn't even qualify for the job in the first place? The bible talks about seasons, seasons of laughter and seasons of pain, but most importantly it speaks about every promise that God has made to his people. He will always keep his promises, so there's no need to doubt whether or not God will bless you.

My favorite promise of all comes from Jeremiah 29:11, *"For I know the plans I have for you", declares the Lord, "plans to prosper you and not to harm you, plans to give you hope and a future."*

Interestingly enough, this promise is always misconstrued and taken out of context. Here's the backstory behind that scripture: the Israelites were in exile because of their disobedience to God, however, Jeremiah told them to settle in exile, build houses, establish families and live a life of freedom while in so-called captivity. Jeremiah also told them they had seventy years of this life, so he encouraged them to enjoy it. Although the Israelites weren't where they wanted to be they still had the opportunity to enjoy life. The same applies to you. Although you may not have the car you want, enjoy the car you have now. Yes, you are working a regular 9-5; enjoy it. Build relationships, and use those resources to help you develop and build the business you want in the future.

I was in a serious spiritual rut in 2013. I felt like God had forgotten about me. I was broke, facing eviction, in a bad relationship and so disconnected from God, I barely prayed. I never opened my Bible or acknowledged God's presence. It was a serious struggle to get me inside the church around those phony, judgmental Christians. I was so angry with God that I didn't want to have anything to do with Him. It wasn't until I realized that although I was in a tough situation, I served a God who could turn anything around. I realized that it was my season to go through the storm. I learned to accept that I was having a hard time and that this hard time was only temporary. I began to thank God for everything, good and bad, much and little, sweet and sour. I let God back into my heart by starting to pray again, reading the word and inviting God to be a part of my daily living. I also gave up one of my favorite things in the world: sex. I told God that if he doesn't do anything else for me, his grace is sufficient enough.

Listen, you must learn to be content in your current situation until God tells you to move. Trust and believe that until you grow stronger in your faith, God won't transition you to the next level. Think about it, you wouldn't even be spiritually ready to receive that blessing yet. Of course, the plan is to prosper you, give you hope, not to harm you and to give you a bright future, but that's after you've learned the lessons God is trying to teach you. You will undergo spiritual warfare on a daily basis, but the purpose is to make your faith stronger. When you get weary, take a look at these eight promises that God always keeps.

Dana Marie: Eight Powerful Promises of God

- **God promises to be faithful!**

  Every promise that God makes he keeps. He will continue to be faithful to you no matter what you've done. He forgives you faithfully, loves you faithfully and blesses you faithfully. Even when it seems like God's not right by your side, he remains true and just. When you feel like he's changing remember that God is the same God today, yesterday and forever more.

  > *"For the Lord is good and his love endures forever, his faithfulness continues through all generations."*
  > Psalms 100:5

- **God promises to give you strength in the time of struggle.**

  Life comes with ups and downs, but God is always there to help you through those challenging times. He will give you supernatural strength to deal with life – divorce, job loss, depression and whatever else is not too big for the God in you. God will remind you that he is always there with you, in the good times and bad times, he's there waiting to take the fear away and equip you with the power to defeat the enemy. Remember that you can do all things through Christ.

  > *"So do not fear, for I am with you; do not be dismayed, for I am your God. I will strengthen you and help you; I will uphold you with my righteous right hand."*
  > Isaiah 41:10

- **God promises to supply your needs.**

  Oftentimes we worry about our basic needs being met. What will I eat? What will I wear? But God said that you don't need to worry about those things. He knows what you need and will give you everything you need to live out his purpose for your life. If the birds don't have to worry about life why should you worry; aren't you more important than the birds. You ain't got no worries!

> *"And my God will meet all your needs according to the riches of his glory in Christ Jesus."*
> Philippians 4:19

- **God promises to guide your path.**

The world will continuously challenge your walk with Christ. As you become closer to God the devil will try even harder to tempt you, but God is here to lead and guide you every step of the way. Invite the holy spirit into your daily decision-making process, so you can be clear that you are following the footsteps of Christ. Trusting in the Lord in all your ways will help you stay on the straight and narrow path of God's will. Keep your eyes on God and he will lead you.

> *"I will instruct you and teach you in the way you should go; I will counsel you with my loving eye on you."*
> Psalms 32:8

- **God promises to love you unconditionally.**

Real love is sacrificial. God loves you so much that he sent his son to die for your sins even when you didn't deserve it. God continuously shows you grace, giving you stuff you don't deserve, and mercy, preventing you from getting the wrath you do deserve because he loves you. God continues to bless you with life, food, money, cars, houses, opportunities and so much more only because he loves you. Continue to thank him for his unfailing, unconditional love because he didn't have to give it to you.

> *"But God demonstrates his own love for us in this:*
> *While we were yet sinners, Christ died for us."*
> Romans 5:8

- **God promises to provide an abundant living.**

    Your life as a Christian isn't supposed to be boring. You were created to enjoy life. As the slogan goes, "Eat, Drink and Be Merry," the plan that God has for you will consist of balance. Every day of the week is not supposed to be dedicated to the church. Live a little. Travel the world, make some friends, create a bucket list, but most importantly live the best life you have now. Tomorrow isn't promised so the longer you wait to live life the shorter you'll have to experience life. Live today, God's abundance is waiting for you.

> *"But seek first his kingdom and his righteousness, and all these things will be given to you as well. Therefore do not worry about tomorrow, for tomorrow will worry about itself. Each day has enough trouble of its own."*
> Matthew 6:33-34

- **God promises to forgive!**

    Whether you were a mass murderer or cursed out your cousin for eating your leftovers in the fridge, God still gives you the same forgiveness, if you sincerely ask. God is patiently waiting for you to repent your sins and try every day to live a righteous life. Once your sins are forgiven God removes the guilt, so you no longer have to beat yourself up about something you did ten years or ten minutes ago. When your past tries to haunt you remember that God has already forgiven you. If you are sincere in your desire to be forgiven, your deliverance and healing process will begin.

> *"If my people, who are called by my name, will humble themselves and pray and seek my face and turn from their*

wicked ways, then I will hear from heaven, and I will
forgive their sin and will heal their land."
2 Chronicles 7:14

- **God promises to grant you eternal life!**

When the earth passes away, isn't a blessing to know that you will still have eternal life. God has prepared a place for all who believe in him to go after life on earth called Heaven. Don't worry about death because for a believer there is no death. You will forever have the privilege to bask in the glorious presence of God. It's the ultimate "turn up" for those that like to party. When you wholeheartedly follow Jesus, hell, a burning hot fire pit, where non-believers are sent to be with the Devil, is not an option. Stop worrying about life after death, because God already promised you eternal life.

"Therefore, there is now no condemnation for
those who are in Christ Jesus, because through
Christ Jesus the law of the Spirit who gives life has
set you free from the law of sin and death."
Romans 8:1-2

As you reflect on all the spiritual attacks you've undergone so far, feeling alone, desolated from God, feeling weak and spiritually unprepared to take on the devil, I want you to remember that you are more than a conqueror (See Romans 8:37). I encourage you to strengthen your relationship with God, and then walk with confidence as you live a life full of freedom, embracing and accepting every obstacle that comes your way. You have authority over the devil. You can demand that he leaves you alone as you walk closer to God.

"If you resist the devil he will flee"
James 4:7

Once you are free spiritually every other aspect of your life will seem much easier to dominate. When you are called by God to be great it's the devil's job to stop you at any cost. With all your might, stop him before he even gets started. Live life free, spiritually!

Mental Freedom

CHAPTER FOUR

TAINTED, BUT STILL FORGAVE

I remember it was winter. It was cold and the house quiet as a mouse. My sister was asleep on the bottom bunk. I was in my bed on the top bunk having the best of eight-year-old dreams about unicorns and rainbows and Afro puff superheroes. Then suddenly, I felt a heavy hand caressing my butt, then groping it, fondling inside it, licking and kissing. He made his way down to my feet and with such passion he sucked toe after toe. I was jolted; awoken by someone violating me. I laid there still, the tears rolling down my eyes like a flowing river, my innocence drifting away. I tried to pretend to still be sleep, moving as if I was taunted by a bad dream, but my molester did not stop. Although my sister was present in the room I couldn't open my mouth to scream. I was numb. I felt tainted; worthy of disgrace and ashamed.

The abuse went on night after night intensifying with every encounter. Every day I'd wake up in the morning encouraging myself to tell my mom, but I just couldn't muster up the strength. The abuse wasn't just physical. No, it was way more than that; it was mental abuse too. My molester was constantly telling me how ugly I was, how fat I was getting, how stupid I was and how worthless I would always be. Most times I believed what he was saying. Then I'd have moments when I couldn't understand how I was so worthless to him if he insisted on molesting me every night. When the lights were out his obsession with molesting me proved that I was his weakness; his sickness made me irresistible in every way. Psychologically I was all messed up, I thought God had left me. I began to internalize every word my abuser said. I believed that I was worthless. I felt tainted. I felt disgusting. I lost my innocence. I lost my youth. I lost my sanity.

Two years passed and my molester left the house. For a moment, I thought I was free. I was wrong. Not only did a male violate me, two females turned around and did the same exact thing when he left. I was told that if I told, no one would believe me, so I didn't tell. I began to think that it was normal for people to touch me inappropriately. So much so that in school if a boy grabbed my butt I didn't even tell the teacher. I had no sense of defense because I was so weak. I didn't feel like I mattered because no one ever asked for my opinion anyway. They touched me without my permission, so what good was it to say what I wanted and how I felt after the fact.

There was no one I trusted so I distanced myself from everyone. It's a terrible feeling to grow up in a house full of people and yet feel so alone. Family game nights began to fade, family prayer was a mockery and Sunday dinner had diminished. I hated my life; I hated who I was and the things that happened to me. I was a slave to my thoughts, living my life in fear with no one to turn to. Although he said in his word that he will never leave me or forsake me, (See Deuteronomy 31:8) I was certain God had abandoned me, so I abandoned him.

It took me eight years to finally tell my mother what happened to me. I was sixteen years old at the time. I had buried my past hurts so far down, I was an expert at masking the pain. See, I was known for always laughing and joking around, but no one knew that it was only to keep from crying.

Soon it became too much to keep down and I decided to rid myself of the pain forever, but the self-inflicted slits to my wrist didn't do it. I only bled temporary relief. The countless pills I swallowed didn't take me to peaceful, eternal rest. Instead, I gagged and choked up pill after pill. The belt strap around my neck didn't pull tight enough to leave me breathless. Fortunately, my lungs never failed me. After my third suicide attempt, I finally decided it was time to tell.

My mother's reaction was heartbreaking. She wondered why I didn't tell her sooner. I looked her in the face and shrugged my shoulders thinking it was the dumbest question she could have ever asked. I didn't know why. All I knew is that I was ready to tell at *that* moment. My mother told me that I needed to forgive all the people who abused me. I could have slapped the black off her. Forgiving them was the last thing on my mind. I thought I was doing the right thing by ignoring and masking it. Little did I know I was just damaging myself even more.

Later that night I begin to pray for the first time in about two years. I said, "God, do you remember me? It's Dana. Why did you do this to me? What did I do to deserve this treatment? I am so angry with you, Lord. You abandoned me. Why? You let them take my innocence when you had the power to stop them. Why?"

The room was still. I didn't hear the mysterious voice that I expected to hear, but I did feel a sense of peace and his full presence as I wept every tear I'd been holding in for eight years. It had been a long time since I invited God in my life again because I blamed him for everything that happened to me. God could have either prevented it from happening or just wiped my abusers out, but he didn't. I had to come to terms with the fact that God gives all of us free will to make choices. My abusers chose to do what they did to me, not God. As hard as it was to believe God was still sovereign even in that situation. I knew that he would turn it around for my good because all things work together for good for those who love God and are called according to his purposes. (See Romans 8:28) He is a loving and forgiving God who gives all of his children mercy, even when we feel like they don't deserve it. So, if God could forgive, I knew I could too.

> *"You, Lord, are forgiving and good, abounding*
> *in love to all who call to you."*
> Psalms 86:5

I realized that forgiveness was one of the keys to my mental freedom. To begin the healing process, I needed to forgive the people who hurt me just as Christ forgave me. I also needed to forgive myself for turning my back on God. I didn't know where to begin or how to do it, but I knew I needed to forgive those who hurt me. I understood that forgiving them didn't mean *they* were sorry for what they did to me and I had to be okay with that. I was genuinely forgiving my molesters because firstly, I wanted to make my life right with God. If we don't forgive others Christ won't forgive us. (See Matthew 6:15) Secondly, I was so tired of feeling tainted. My molesters had a mental control over me long after they stopped abusing me. I couldn't take it anymore, so I set out on a journey to heal and forgive.

You probably have a similar story. I'm sure you can relate to having been victimized, blamed, and/or let down by the people you love; losing yourself in the process. To begin your mental freedom, you must forgive, let go and move forward. The agony of your tainted thoughts is keeping you captive in a mental prison. There's no manual on forgiveness, but I've found that acknowledging, accepting and letting go the pain helped me tremendously. Before I forgave my abusers, I would literally feel sick to my stomach every time I thought about them. My heart would skip multiple beats and my world felt so empty. I promise you once I forgave them, with a sincere heart, I felt a sense of peace that came over me. I felt my healing taking place. I felt in control of my life.

Dana Marie's Tips for Fervent Forgiving

- **Understand that what happened is already done.**

  You must realize that time has already passed and cannot be undone. I'm not trying to discredit whatever happened to you. However, I need you to understand that you can't change it or take it back. God doesn't want you to keep dwelling on the past hurts because he has so much planned for you in the future. Your past pain is directly correlated with your future gain.

  > *"Forget the former things; do not dwell on the past.*
  > *See, I am doing a new thing! Now it springs up; do you*
  > *not perceive it? I am making a way in the wilderness and*
  > *streams in the wasteland."*
  > Isaiah 43:18-19

- **Explore the emotions underlying the situation you experienced.**

  It's okay to cry, scream, or roll around on the floor until you feel like you can breathe again. Stop beating yourself up for having moments like this you can't explain. It's normal to feel overwhelmed, aggressive, and angry. What better way to take your frustrations out then on a pillow. Just be sure not to stay angry, ask God to change your heart and heal the pain, before the anger consumes you.

  > *"In your anger do not sin": Do not let*
  > *the sun go down while you are still angry,*
  > *and do not give the devil a foothold."*
  > Ephesians 4:26-27

- **Assess the situation as thoroughly as you can.**

  Examine what you may or may not have done to cause the situation to happen. Were you the quarrelsome wife who constantly bashed your husband, so he stepped out on you seeking validation? Were you the man who used to be on the streets dealing drugs, committing heinous crimes and now the victim's family retaliated? Sometimes our current pain is the repercussions of our past actions. However, if you played no part in what happened, like me, an innocent little girl being taken advantage of, then I'm sure your biggest question is "Why me?". Honestly, the only thing I can tell you is that God has a purpose for your pain. It's coming!

> *"I, even I, am he who blots out your transgressions,*
> *for my own sake, and remembers your sins no more.*
> *Review the past for me, let us argue the matter together;*
> *state the case for your innocence."*
> Isaiah 43:25-26

- **Write your pain down on paper.**
  Write down everything that's painful in your life. Carefully read your list. Let it sink in. Then rip the paper into as many pieces as possible and throw it straight in the trash. You'll see your pain written on paper, which provides visual clarity. You can physically cast the pain away which helps to let go. These actions help to provide a little more relief because you are taking physical action.

> *"Then the Lord said to Moses, "Write this on a*
> *scroll as something to be remembered and make sure that*
> *Joshua hears it, because I will completely blot out the name*
> *of Amalek from under heaven."*
> Exodus 17:14

- **If possible, have a conversation with your offender to express yourself.**

Talk to your offender, let them know they hurt you and tell them you forgive them. Understand, he or she may not be sorry, but that's not your fight. Your purpose for this task is to get the pain off your chest, so you can live a free life. God instructs us to forgive others even when they aren't sorry. As a believer, you are to live like Christ and if Christ can forgive you for all the lies you told and sins you committed against him, then I'm sure you can work to forgive your offender. It will be a challenge, but God is with you every step of the way.

> *"If another believer sins against you, go privately and point out the offense. If the other person listens and confesses it, you have won that person back."*
> Matthew 18:15 NLT

- **Think and do Godly things continuously to refocus.**

When you began to think about the uncle who molested you or the girl who broke your heart do things to change your thoughts. Reading, exercising, watching your favorite show or even getting dressed up to "hit the town." Let's say you are so drained that you can't find the strength to physically do anything, well then think positive thoughts. You can think of your favorite bible verse or sun rays shining over the clear crystal ocean. Self-pity can be crippling, so stop thinking "Why me?" God doesn't want you to feel hopeless, for he is the almighty God who makes all things work together for your good.

> *"You will keep in perfect peace those whose minds are steadfast, because they trust in you."*
> Isaiah 26:3

- **Talk with someone you can trust about the situation to get it off your mind.**

Expressing your feelings to family members and friends may or may not be the best option. They might have bias opinions about the situation because of familial ties. Be sure that you can trust them before you consider them as someone you can talk to. I recommend finding a therapist or a good Christian counselor that will provide you judgment-free opportunities to express your feelings. You want someone with a heart for God, good intentions and a sincere desire to listen and provide biblical advice if needed.

> *"A good man brings good things out of the good stored up in his heart, and an evil man brings evil things out of the evil stored up in his heart. For the mouth speaks what the heart is full of."*
> Luke 6:45

- **Move on and stop worrying about them.**

    The people who hurt you are probably living their lives with no remorse. You should, too. Don't allow them to continue to have the same control over you as they did in the past. You have the power to forgive, let go and move on. They may seem to be living the good life, new car, better job, beautiful spouse, but God has a plan. God said vengeance belongs to him, he will give them exactly what they sowed. (See Romans 12:19) Stop allowing their "happy life" make you feel inferior. God got you! He will seek revenge on your behalf, just stay faithful to him.

    > *"Don't worry about the wicked or envy those who do wrong. For like grass, they soon fade away. Like spring flowers, they soon wither. Trust in the LORD and do good. Then you will live safely in the land and prosper."*
    > Psalms 37:1-3 NLT

One of the greatest things about forgiving someone is that it frees you. That person no longer has control over your mind once you let them go. The manipulative, abusive, demonic person from your past won't affect how you react to present situations. You will be able to love again, trust again, feel again and live life again because you're regaining control over your mind. You're one step closer to living life mentally free.

CHAPTER FIVE

STOP THE STIGMA. GO GET HELP!

Growing up, I hated that I ended up being a statistic. My father was a revolving door in my life. When he did show up he was either drunk or having one of his mental breakdowns. He never told me he loved me as a child. He didn't come to my dance performances even when I bought the ticket for him myself. All I could remember is the broken promises that played on repeat in my head. I remember the arguments and fights he picked with my mother just because she wouldn't aid his drug addiction.

Ironically, he was the most loved man in our neighborhood, but behind closed doors, he was a monster. Although he never physically or sexually abused me, I was mentally scarred from all the pain and broken promises. He wasn't there like I needed him to be. He was either too high on drugs or stumbling from alcohol to love anyone to full capacity. I wanted more from him, but he couldn't give. I knew God was my father and that he was the one who supplies my needs, but I still needed my biological father to be there for me. I considered myself fatherless and, like most fatherless girls, I grew up searching for a father figure in a man not realizing the damage to come.

I was seventeen years old when I started working in my neighborhood's most popular barbershop and beauty salon. The place was spacious with mirrors and bright spotlights from floor to ceiling. The shop was separated into two large sections, the barbers chatted about sports and money in the front, while the lady's gossiped about celebrities and men in the back. They were joined together in the center of the shop by the shampoo bowls that served both the male and female customers. I needed a part-time job to cover my expenses for my freshman year in college. My mother didn't have the money and my father couldn't get himself together, so I had to make a way to get the money I needed to survive and buy books, toiletries, food, etc. Even the bible says if you don't work you don't eat (See 2 Thessalonians 3:10). My first day walking in I got the job as a shampoo girl and I started that same day.

Since I was the new girl I had won the attention of the barbers and the curiosity of the hair stylist and other shampoo girls. Little did they know I wasn't paying any attention to any of them because I had one goal in mind, money. One spring day while working at the shop I had a severe allergy attack, my eyes were bloodshot red, nose running and my face as puffy as a blowfish. This mysterious barber watched me as I scratched my eyeballs out and use the entire roll of toilet paper to blow the snot from my nose. He showed me the compassion and care that a father would show his daughter. I was sitting in the shampoo chair waiting for my next client when he walked up to me with a Rite Aid bag. He said nothing as he placed the bag in my lap. With the little eyesight I had left, I peeped in the bag and saw Zyrtec, a nasal spray, and Puff tissues. I smiled from ear to ear as I rushed to use the medicine to gain relief from my allergy attack. One person had finally caught my bloodshot red, itchy eye.

Over the next few weeks, we began to establish a solid friendship. He began to stimulate my mind with the intellectual conversations we'd have about life. His protective instincts made me feel safe enough to love again and be happy. He showered me with all the essentials I needed for my college endeavor. It was like Christmas and Santa had bought me a computer, printer, brand new wardrobe, books and a plethora of hygiene products. Prom time and graduation came around and he was there grinning the whole time. He was truly like the father I never had. I longed for a father for so long and he filled that void. He gave me advice about life and men, he took care of me when I was sick, he made sure I had "spending money" to go out with friends and most importantly he was supportive. Once legal, 18 years old, we transitioned into a romantic relationship. Two months before graduation, we started dating seriously, then I moved in with him.

At 19, he proposed to me inside a tiny Moroccan restaurant and we had a baby girl, Jaisa, one year later. Although I had some reservations about accepting - I was a freshman at Kutztown University, he was 14 years older than me and I wanted to move to London to pursue a career in TV - I still said yes. I was so caught up in filling this void of emptiness in my life that my spirit of discernment was completely off. He was Muslim and I was Christian, which according to the word isn't what God intends for his people.

> *"Do not be yoked together with unbelievers. For what do righteousness and wickedness have in common? Or what fellowship can light have with darkness?"*
> 2 Corinthians 6:14

I didn't realize that my husband was trying to mold me into his perfect wife, changing everything about me, demeaning my opinions and manipulating my decisions. He was verbally and physically abusive. He would choke and man-handle me because of his own personal frustrations. He committed adultery by cheating on me with women even younger than me. He even attacked me while our daughter was in my arms in broad daylight. We had a plethora of heated physical arguments. One argument I was thrown down the steps of my home. The next, I was locked in a house and pushed around, another, I was dodging punches. To be quite honest, the dysfunctional part of me enjoyed it. I was so mentally screwed up from watching my father do the exact same things that I thought this was normal. I felt dysfunctional when things were functioning correctly. I yearned for the mental torture. I needed the physical pain. His harsh words brought back old hurts about being molested and fatherless. I was spiraling downhill from all the pain, new and old, at a very fast pace with no breaks to stop me. At that time, my only choice was to stay and die mentally or divorce him and move on. I chose to get a divorce. I knew I needed to separate myself from my husband but moving on was difficult. I was too weak to handle this myself, but I also had too much pride to ask for help.

> *"Where there is strife, there is pride, but wisdom*
> *is found in those who take advice."*
> Proverbs 13:10

I was constantly depressed. One day, I remember bargaining with God. "God, if I take these pills, the whole bottle, and I live, I will find someone to help me. I'll go to therapy, God."

I was a woman of my word. I started calling clinics and hospitals to find a behavioral health therapist that could help me. At 21, I was going through a divorce, depression, and once again, attempted suicide because I was mentally imprisoned. My pessimistic thoughts made me lose all hope. I couldn't fight this fight alone. I knew I needed help. I was tired of being an emotional wreck all the time, so I committed to seeing a therapist. My therapist provided me with the support to initiate my recovery. If it weren't for God sparing my life I wouldn't have this testimony. Not only did he spare my life, but he put highly trained professionals there to guide me through depression, suicidal ideations, and attempts.

There will be overwhelming situations in life that may be difficult to navigate alone. Sometimes the road ahead looks so bleak we can't even see ourselves taking one step forward. That's when it's time to ask for help. There are professionals out there equipped to support you. The process of finding the right therapist and going may be a bit intimidating at first for so many reasons. According to a study conducted by Ward, Wiltshire, Detry, and Brown in 2013 black people hold beliefs related to stigma, psychological openness, and help-seeking, which in turn affects their coping behaviors with black men in particularly concerned about the stigma (Mental Health Alliance). These fears include the fear of stigma and being called "crazy". Fear of the unknown and having to attend therapy for a long time. Or even the fear of being judged by society for needing help and placed on "crazy people" medication. All these things are legitimate fears, however, if you want healing, you must overcome these fears and start the process. Here are some tips to help you find the right fit for you and your personal needs.

Dana Marie's Tips for Thriving at Therapy

- **Forget the social stigmas, it's okay to get help.**

  I never understood why it's frowned upon, especially in the African American community, to go to therapy. Only about one-quarter of African Americans seek mental health care, compared to 40% of whites (NAMI). Therapy is intended to relieve and heal you. Sometimes your problems are too big to handle yourself. God placed highly trained, judgment-free professionals who will listen to your story, help you cope and guide you down the road to recovery. God can handle your issue without a problem, but he also puts people in place to do his work. Good therapists are a gift from God, utilize them.

  > *"Every good and perfect gift is from above,*
  > *coming down from the Father of the heavenly lights,*
  > *who does not change like shifting shadows."*
  > James 1:17

- **Do your research!**

  You may have to find a therapist outside your neighborhood. Look for the best of the best to help you get through your mental breakdowns. It's always great to look up your therapist credentials and years of experience. You may even find testimonials from people who were treated by the therapist you're considering. You can also ask your friends and family for suggestions. There is always some apprehension in choosing a therapist but use your best discernment.

  > *"So give your servant a discerning heart to govern your*
  > *people and to distinguish between right and wrong.*
  > *For who is able to govern this great people of yours?"*
  > 1 Kings 3:9

- **Know your rights.**

    Your therapist must treat you with dignity and respect. He or she is sworn to secrecy unless you're suicidal or homicidal. You should not be discriminated against based on your age, race, or illness. If at any moment you feel that you're unfairly treated, if you're receiving services at a hospital, contact the Director of Behavioral Health or, if it's private practice, contact The Citizens Commission on Human Rights. You're entitled your rights, but it's your job to exercise them.

    > *"You must teach these things and encourage the believers to do them. You have the authority to correct them when necessary, so don't let anyone disregard what you say."*
    > Titus 2:15 NLT

- **Utilize emergency services for immediate support.**

    Sometimes you may need to talk with your therapist immediately, but they may not be available in that case there are several options for you. You can call 911 to have the ambulance escort you to the nearest Crisis Center, a place where people go to get help if they are experiencing an immediate crisis. You can call the National Suicide Hotline at 1- 800-273-TALK, if you are experiencing suicidal thoughts and/or actions. If you're overwhelmed and in a panic call 1-800- 64-PANIC. If you still feel hopeless, remember that prayer works, talk to God about your problems. He will always listen.

    > *"Give your burdens to the LORD, and he will take care of you. He will not permit the godly to slip and fall."*
    > Psalms 55:22 NLT

- **Exercise your power to change therapists.**

    If you don't feel connected to the one you have, remember, you are not legally bound to one therapist. With your consent, your records can be transferred to the therapist of your choice if you feel like you aren't getting the help you need. Remember the therapist is there for you. A therapist's purpose is to do everything in their power to help you navigate the challenges of life without making you feel discriminated against and/or judged. You should feel the sincerity and a genuine connection. If you feel they aren't doing that, then move on. There should be no animosity between you and your therapist. This is one of the places you should receive peace.

> *"Let us therefore make every effort to do what leads to peace and to mutual edification."*
> Romans 14:19

- **Consistency is key.**

Stay committed to getting the help you need. Continue to go to your appointments. Make your mental wellness a priority in your life. If money becomes an issue check with your employer to see if they offer an Employee Assistance Program. These types of programs provide support for employees dealing with adverse life issues that directly affect their work, health, and well-being. There are sliding scale therapists, who allow you to pay the fee according to your income. The less money you make the less you'll pay. Governmental programs like Medicaid also offer behavioral health benefits at no cost to their recipients. Do whatever you need to do to stay committed!

> *"Let us hold unswervingly to the hope we profess, for he who promised is faithful."*
> Hebrews 10:23

- **Be patient with yourself.**

    One therapy session isn't going to take all your problems away. Allow yourself time to heal and time for the sessions to work. Your problems most likely didn't occur instantly, so why should your recovery? You will feel better in time. Don't rush the process, trust the process. It may not take two months to heal you might need two years. It may not take one session a week you might need three a week. You might even need medication to help support the process. The point is to be patient and take your time with healing. You don't want to relapse because you didn't take the time to thoroughly heal. It's a marathon, not a race.

    > *"But they who wait for the L*ORD *shall renew their strength; they shall mount up with wings like eagles; they shall run and not be weary; they shall walk and not faint."*
    > Isaiah 40:31 ESV

- **Recognize you're getting stronger each day.**

    Sometimes you might not know what you need to talk about and how it will heal you, but the fact that you made it to your appointment shows progress. As you and the therapist work to uncover some of the struggles in your life remember that you are one step closer to fully healing. Take the advice you receive from your therapist and use it to build upon the small strength you already have. You can do it. You will get through it. You'll get stronger one day at a time.

    > *"But the Lord is faithful, and he will strengthen you and protect you from the evil one."*
    > 2 Thessalonians 3:3

As Christians, we are taught that God will handle all of our problems. Yes, that is true, but sometimes he uses people to intervene on his behalf. You should never feel like you don't have anyone to turn to during life's rough patches. Therapists are here to serve you and to help you recover from the obstacles that weigh you down. God strategically gave them the gift of counsel to help guide you through life's challenges. Swallow your pride and do what's necessary for your mental well-being. Someone is always there to help, you just have to be willing to receive. Your freedom depends on you.

CHAPTER SIX

RENEW YOUR THOUGHTS: POSITIVITY ONLY!

For me, 2012 was supposed to be my last year alive, but God said otherwise. I was struggling to cope with experiencing molestation as a child, growing up fatherless, being domestically abuse throughout my marriage and getting a divorce. Once I forgave all the people who hurt me I thought I'd receive instantaneous healing, but there was very little healing progress. I dedicated portions of my day to mental therapy and I still didn't see any changes. I prayed every night, read the word, but I still didn't feel better. I still thought I was worthless. I still didn't feel good enough. I still thought I was inadequate. Negative thoughts constantly raced through my mind day in and day out. I would think things like, "You deserved what happened to you. You will never be worth anything. You are so ugly. You are so fat. No one wants a tainted, sexually abused single mother!"

Those thoughts plagued my life so much so that I believed every word. I had no confidence and no self-esteem. I didn't place value on my life or myself. I pretended like I wasn't suffering, but deep down inside I was still lost, just waiting to be found.

One day, I went for what started out as a neighborhood stroll just to clear my mind and ending up being four miles away from my house. When I looked up, I noticed that trash filled the sidewalks and graffiti plagued the walls. Children were running in and out of the street playing curb ball and jumping rope as the smell of BBQ hit me stronger than ever. It was a typical summer day in the hood. The screams of drug dealing men barricading the corner store became louder and more aggressive as I traveled to my unknown destination.

"Yooooo!"

"Hey, sexy!"

"Shorty with the fatty."

To them, I was just one of those burgers on the grill just waiting to be devoured like another piece of meat. I shook my head from side to side in disgust, as I tried to ignore their calls. They continued to yell louder and louder, trying harder and harder to get my attention. The more they yelled the more uncomfortable I became because deep down inside I felt undesirable. I was ashamed of my body and insecure about myself. Desperately trying to escape I turned the corner, crossed the street and hid behind the bush in the new community garden. I was reminded of my childhood, being taken advantage of, violated and I was scared it would happen again.

The screams faded and I took a deep breath as I proceeded to walk through the garden.

"Hello, Queen! You look very beautiful. I'm praying that your day is as wonderful as you are!"

I turned my head to see where the kind words had come from. There was a handsome brother standing not too far from me, grinning from ear to ear. I went from hearing sounds of hungry, barking dogs to a symphonic harp. His voice gave me chills. This man stimulated my mind with his affirming words. With a gullible heart, I listen to the kind words he spoke and then I gave him my phone number to continue the conversation once I returned home from my walk.

We talked on the phone every day, from sunrise to sunset, for about two weeks. He was so charming. He told me how beautiful, amazing, intelligent and priceless I was. I remember blushing and telling him to stop and that I wasn't all that. I felt a sense of worth speaking to him. I looked for him to provide me with the confidence to look in the mirror and accept myself. I yearned for his validation. I was desperate for his approval. He had me wrapped around his finger and there was nothing I wouldn't do for him.

A month went by and the mask that he wore began to fade. He started to show his true personality. I'm guessing he was getting tired of giving me so many accolades without receiving anything in return. We had finally planned to go out on a date. He would come to my mother's house and we'd talk outside, but for the most part, we never left the steps. He told me he was taking me out to a nice restaurant, so I put on a little black dress. My makeup was flawless and my hair nicely pressed. When I stepped in his black Mercedes Benz, I was overwhelmed by the New Car scent while Luther Vandross softly played in the background. We drove from Philadelphia to Delaware. He pulled up to an apartment building, I looked confused because I thought we were going out to dinner. I didn't realize his plan was to cook dinner for me. As naive as I could be I stepped out the car, my heels clashing against the concrete, curiosity clouding my head and I walked into his apartment.

 His apartment looked like it was hit by a tsunami, clothes, shoes, drugs, and trash everywhere. It didn't take me long to realize that there was never any intention to take me out or to ever cook me dinner. After saying no over five times my Mr. Nice Guy forced me to have sex with him, violently throwing me on the bed while climbing on top of me. I knew this was rape, but I just couldn't muster up enough courage to scream the word "stop" loud enough. I was scared that if I screamed he'd kill me, after all, no one knew where I was. My body stiffened like it did back when I was eight as he continued to take advantage of me. When he was done, he said, "Nice. Get dressed, beautiful."

 I was confused, he had just raped me, but gave me a compliment and called me beautiful…What? On the way home, I didn't say a word, my mind was racing. Anger, rage, and pity, fear was running the 100-meter dash back in forth in my head. At one point I wanted to attack him in the car but knew I wasn't strong enough to take him on if he retaliated. Was I a victim or did I owe him this for all the kind words he'd said to me? I looked over at him, but he showed no interest. He continued to bob his head as he listened to Luther Vandross, not once acknowledging my presence in the car.

 Just when I thought it couldn't get any worse, it did. He never stopped calling, he showed up at my house and forced his way into my everyday life. His manipulative and controlling ways forced me to give in to his pressures because he would feed me the "You're so beautiful. You're amazing. You're my baby," that I ignored the fact he'd raped me. I was his personal sex slave and he was my pimp. He explained my hourly rate was $100 per hour. I was so scared and weak that I agreed to his insane plan. I couldn't imagine losing the one person that praised me so much, so I did anything he wanted me to do. I'd already felt worthless, so when he put a $100 value on me I thought, "At least I'm worth something now."

As the praises continued, the sexual acts increased, splits, flips, twirls, curls, anything for "Daddy." I tried so hard to please him every encounter we had, but soon the emptiness began to grow inside my heart. When he'd notice my distance during sex he'd bark vulgar commands, demanding me to go harder or faster to please him. I'd try with all my might but it just wasn't good enough for him. Out of frustration, his kind words turned to harsh phrases, his gentle gestures turned to aggression and just that quick I was nothing to him. Every sexual experience got worse and worse, I knew I had to let it go soon.

One time after sex he yelled, "You know I'm tired of you not treating Daddy right. You're not getting $100 today, you only deserve $25. And you're lucky I'm giving you that." Right then and there, I knew I reached my breaking point. He threw the old raggedy twenty-dollar bill on the bed, then one by one dropped dollar bills to the floor. I jumped up from to bed to try to catch each one before they fell eventually falling to my knees scraping up all the dignity I had left dollar by dollar. Quietly mumbling to myself, "Enough is enough. I'm done with this. This will be your last time." During the ride home, I made a promise to myself to leave him alone and go back to God.

When I returned home I ran straight to my room, slamming the door behind me falling to my knees. My river was dry because the tears refused to fall. I realized that I once again abandoned God. I needed to reconnect with him so that I could remember who I was in Christ. I prayed long and hard. I asked God to forgive me for all that I'd done. I asked him to help me forgive this man and let him go. God told me that I am somebody. He said this man didn't have the power to assess or change my value. I began to think positive thoughts about who I was and who I aspired to be. I'd say, "Dana you're priceless., Dana, you're amazing. Dana, you're bigger than this. Dana, you can do all things through Christ."

For weeks I continued to invite God into my thoughts. I wanted him to control everything that came to my mind, and he did. I was set free.

Just like me, your freedom will come once you change your mindset. The process of changing all my negative thoughts to positive, affirming spoken words is what saved me. I started to regain mental freedom by transforming negativity to positivity. Despite what I felt inside I just began to speak life to myself. Every time a negative thought crossed my mind I would literally shake my head then think something positive. For instance, the thought, "You will never get out of this situation," would come to mind and I would immediately say, "I am the painter of my life and I have the power to create a masterpiece." I developed a strong, solid rebuttal for every negative thought that came to my mind. I was determined to change my thoughts so that I could free myself from this mental prison that had full control of my life. Here are a few tips that will help you transform your thoughts to create a healthier, positive mindset.

Dana Marie's Tips for Transformative Thoughts

- **Change the way you think.**

  You must make a conscious decision to do everything in your power to change your thinking. Make a promise to yourself to change the way you think one thought at a time. Every day you have an opportunity to encourage and inspire yourself, so be specific in what you think. You deserve to have peace of mind, which only comes by transformative thinking.

  "Don't copy the behavior and customs of this world, but let God transform you into a new person by changing the way you think. Then you will learn to know God's will for you, which is good and pleasing and perfect."
  Romans 12:2 NLT

- **Fight every negative thought with a positive one.**

  Don't just think the new positive thought, you have to say it, aloud, to yourself. Speak it! The Bible says the power of life and death lies in the tongue (See Proverbs 18:21). If you can scream it, scream it. Put that positivity into the atmosphere. Speak life to yourself. Speak life to every negative thought and hopeless situation. God has given you the power of the tongue.

  "As it is written: "I have made you a father of many nations. He is our father in the sight of God, in whom he believed—the God who gives life to the dead and calls into being things that were not."
  Romans 4:17

- **Write down your affirmations!**

Be sure to post them all over your house, cubicle and even your car. This creates a visual of positivity. If you see it, you will believe it. Start with these:

a. I am more than enough. My worth is priceless. I will not settle for less.

b. I am no longer operating in fear. I am driven by faith.

c. This too shall pass. I have the power and strength to overcome my situation.

d. My blessing is on the other side of this burden. Keep pushing.

"Let love and faithfulness never leave you; bind them around your neck, write them on the tablet of your heart."
Proverbs 3:3

- **Count your blessings!**

Think of the times in your life when situations could have been worse, but they weren't. Instead of seven negative thoughts a day you only have two. That's a blessing. God has given you so many things, both tangible and intangible that you may or may not have deserved. Grace and mercy are God's greatest gifts. Despite our inconsistencies in serving God he still loves us. You're more blessed than you think, look around you.

"And God will generously provide all you need. Then you will always have everything you need and plenty left over to share with others."
2 Corinthians 9:8 NLT

- **Be grateful for everything you currently have.**

Even if it isn't what you wanted, God will see that you are faithful over a few things and make you the ruler of many. Appreciate the small things like water, soap, hot meals and a place to rest your head at night. Think about the fact that you have life and that God's plan for your life is ultimately prosperity. The more gratitude you have the more you'll appreciate life.

> *"Rejoice always, pray continually, give thanks in all circumstances; for this is God's will for you in Christ Jesus."*
> 1 Thessalonians 5:16-18

- **Pray and meditate daily.**

Take this time out to clear your mind. Listen to some relaxing music or sit in peace and quiet. Meditation has the ability to put your entire body and mind in a state of rest. You can get a break from the hardships of life during your meditation moments. Trust me, it's worth turning off your phone, locking yourself in a quiet room and seeking God without any distractions.

> *"Finally, brothers and sisters, whatever is true, whatever is noble, whatever is right, whatever is pure, whatever is lovely, whatever is admirable—if anything is excellent or praiseworthy—think about such things."*
> Philippians 4:8

- **Avoid people who have a negative and pessimistic view.**

These are the people that always find the fault in everything, failing to realize that everyone is perfectly imperfect. Remember that misery loves company. They will do everything in their power to make you as miserable as them. Beware.

> *"Stay away from a fool, for you will not find knowledge on their lips."*
> Proverbs 14:7

- **Understand that ONLY you have the power to change your thoughts.**

You are strong enough to defeat every doubt, every fear and every inadequacy that crosses your mind. Stand firm and believe in yourself. Every day you wake up is a new day to defeat negativity! Be the victor and conquer your mind!

> *"Throw off your old sinful nature and your former*
> *way of life, which is corrupted by lust and deception.*
> *Instead, let the Spirit renew your thoughts and attitudes.*
> *Put on your new nature, created to be like*
> *God—truly righteous and holy."*
> Ephesians 4:22-24 NLT

The mind is a terrible thing to waste on negativity. You must work extremely hard to fight the strongholds that come to take over your thoughts and feelings. The more focus you are on making Christ the center of your attention the more peace of mind you will have. (See Romans 8:6) As you proactively work to get full control over your mind I want you to be patient with yourself. Start with forgiveness, then transformative thinking, and lastly, go get help. You are one of the millions of people who are battling with anxious thoughts, so why are you isolating yourself? I know life sometimes gets hard, but stop playing the victim and become the victor. You can free yourself mentally because the power of Christ lives in you! (See Romans 8:11)

Relationship Freedom

CHAPTER SEVEN

THE USUAL FAMILY DRAMA

One of my biggest struggles has always been trying to fit in with my family so full of different personalities and values. Although I loved the fact that I had a blended family with eight brothers and sisters, it wasn't always easy. Most of them didn't believe that Jesus was the way nor did they hold him central to their life as I did. As I mentioned before it's a sad thing when you grow up around so many people, but feel so alone. Of course, everyone in my family has their personal story to tell and I won't ever try to take it from them. Every one of my siblings has faced multiple trials and tribulations, some which still control them to this very day. I would often feel obligated to bend over backward, side to side, or jump up and down just to be "super save-a- Bro". I would make everyone else's problems my own. I was creating unnecessary and heavy burdens in my life like debt from loaning siblings money. I was causing a mental overload by trying to solve their problems while struggling to solve my own. It became overwhelming.

I never asked myself if they would do the same things for me in return. In my experiences, most of them have not been the crutch that I needed to pull through. The same dedication that I had to making their lives better wasn't reciprocated. I would sacrifice to make sure they had the things they needed and wanted, but they didn't do the same in return.

Ironically, most of my immediate family thinks I'm this "Perfect Patty," a woman who knows it all and has all her stuff together. I was mommy's favorite, nerdy "Jesus Freak" who did no wrong and had no problems. Honestly, they'll find out more about me after reading this book than they have ever known (sorry guys). For the most part, they don't know too much about me because I was always the "go to" person for them. I couldn't allow them to see me weak, so I never showed or told them how much pressure they made me feel because of all their requests and demands.

As I got older, the requests got larger like, "Take out this loan for me" or "Can I borrow $1000?" Now, because of who I am I did these things without a second thought even though I didn't have it to give. I started overexerting myself for people who were supposed to be there for me but were always too busy to take the time out to simply ask me if I needed anything. It wasn't that I was looking to receive something tangible from them; I was actually hoping that they would notice my pain, my emptiness, and my health issues. I wanted them to see that I was burnt out, and I didn't have anything left to give.

I started to make more conscious decisions that were in my best interest. *No* became my favorite word for a very long time. It wasn't easy saying no because I was ridiculed for it. If I didn't have money to give my brother, I was put on a guilt trip and called "stingy." If I wasn't able to watch my siblings' kids, I was considered selfish. If I challenged them to fight for more in their lives, I was considered rude and snobby. If I gave my truthful opinion and advice, I was considered insensitive and arrogant. I was still extending a helping hand, but it wasn't what they were used to. It wasn't good enough. I was beginning to disappoint the people I cared about most by making the decision to put me first.

A family is the one group of people that you don't choose because they're appointed to you by God for a special purpose. I didn't want to disappoint the one group of people God strategically placed in my life. So, when I couldn't cater to their needs I felt like a failure. See, I was so used to supporting them and making their problems temporarily go away, that I fed off that feeling of being the family "savior". I felt like God had chosen me to be the superhero for my chosen family. But when my superpowers no longer worked, I felt useless to them. All I ever wanted was for them to love me unconditionally, even when I couldn't be the savior anymore. The more hell I began to face in my personal life, the less support I'd get from people God appointed to help lift me up.

Through prayer and discernment, God opened my eyes to see my family for who they truly are. I started to notice most of them were just takers, who honestly didn't care about my feelings or my life, especially if they were in need. When I went through my divorce, I was told to get over it, to move on, and that it was taking too long. When I went through depression I was told to stop acting and that I was being dramatic. I longed for the same attentiveness I gave to every one of my family members, but I couldn't get it.

One of my family members was struggling with addiction to alcohol and opioids. For a long time, I felt bad for all the pain she endured from child rape to domestic violence, to depression. Subconsciously, I would aid her addiction by giving her money when she asked for it, which validated her behavior. I realized that nothing I was doing was helping her heal, physically and mentally, nor did it aid her deliverance. Things had gotten worse: more stealing, lying, prostituting, and using drugs and alcohol. Although it murdered my pride, I had to let her go by giving the situation to God. No more loaning money, no more sympathy, and no more validation. I prayed and fasted and cried out to the only one who could save her. Through this process, I was stuck between embarrassment (because this person was in my family, therefore a representation of me) and guilt (because I couldn't save her in the way that I thought I could). However, if I wanted to see a transformation in her life, I had to set boundaries for our relationship, release the guilt and swallow my pride. As of now, she is getting better, slowly but surely, by the grace of God.

God revealed to me that my family is human, just like me, who falls short of his glory. Your family will most likely make mistakes: some big and some small. They may not always be there for you and will sometimes let you down. Although you may want them to be, they are not perfect people. I thought about how much drama I caused my Father God, yet he still loves and forgives me. I realized that I couldn't get mad at them for being who they were, but I didn't have to be a fool and let them continuously use me (See Proverbs 26:11.) I needed to accept them. God accepts me for who I am and I need to do the same with family. Through acceptance and prayer, I strengthened my relationship with my family, as well as, set healthy boundaries to help me live better. Here are some tips to help you recognize and get through family drama.

Dana Marie's 8 Tips for Functional Family Relationships

- **Realize that you can't save everybody, not even your family.** Stop trying to be the hero in every family situation. Sometimes you may need to take the back burner while they work to sort things out themselves. You're not a superhero! Your family will be okay if *you* don't *personally* save them from every situation. If you step in every time, what room does God have to do a mighty work in their lives? Some situations may be mentally, physically and financially out of your reach, so you must give it to God. Move out the way so *He* can heal, deliver and transform their lives. The true goal is for them to give God the glory, not you!

  "He says, "Be still, and know that I am God; I will be exalted among the nations, I will be exalted in the earth."
  Psalms 46:10

- **Understand that your family won't always be there.**

  There will be times that they may let you down. The money that you let them borrow might not ever get paid back. The advice that you were looking for you might not ever get it. The prayer and fasting that you ask them to partake in with you might not ever happen. Put your trust in God because he will always be there for you. Families are human beings who make mistakes and bad choices just like everyone else.

  "Do not put your trust in princes, in human beings, who cannot save."
  Psalms 146:3

- **Set boundaries and limitations, especially with money.**

  Don't go broke or lose your sanity helping your family. Know when to say yes and when to say no to their request. It's okay to be the go-to person but you must know your limitations, this includes lending out a certain amount of money, only babysitting while the parent is being productive or making yourself unavailable during your moments of self-care. No means no and they should understand that, but you must stick to the boundaries you set.

> *"Just say a simple, 'Yes, I will,' or 'No, I won't.'*
> *Anything beyond this is from the evil one."*
> Matthew 5:37

- **Release the guilt you have from setting boundaries.**

Guilt comes when you feel like you didn't do enough to prevent something from happening. By setting boundaries there may be a lot of things you aren't doing for your family anymore and you need to be ok with it. As I told you before you must let family fall sometimes so they can learn from their mistakes. Don't feel bad about your decision to set boundaries, because God works all things together for good. (See Romans 8:28) Trust what God is doing in the lives of your family even if it seems like they are going through. You've done all that you can do, God must do the rest.

> *"Create in me a pure heart, O God, and renew*
> *a steadfast spirit within me."*
> Psalms 51:10

- **After you've done all you can let your family make their own mistakes.**

It's not your responsibility to be responsible for grown people who you've already extended yourself to multiple times. I know your first inkling is to look out for family, but you can't continue to hinder them from growth. They must learn how to figure things out without you. Allow them to fall, then acknowledge them when they get back up. They must make and learn from their mistakes. If you come to the rescue every time they will always make the same mistakes, expecting you to save them every time.

> *"When he finally came to his senses, he said to himself, 'At home, even the hired servants have food enough to spare, and here I am dying of hunger!"*
> Luke 15:17 NLT

- **Continuously pray for your family and everything they are experiencing.**

The word of God says that some things only come by prayer and fasting. (See Matthew 17:21 NKJV) All you may be able to do to help your family is pray and fast. If you always come to the rescue to save a person, what is there for God to do. Prayer is one of the best ways to help because God hears the prayers of the righteous, therefore he will answer you.

> *"And pray in the Spirit on all occasions with all kinds of prayers and requests. With this in mind, be alert and always keep on praying for all the Lord's people."*
> Ephesians 6:18

- **Forgive those family members who hurt you.**

Let go of the pain and begin your healing process. I know it's hard because your family is supposed to be there for you. These are the people God entrusted with your life, to lead and guide you on the right path. But don't forget that they aren't perfect people. They make bad choices, just like you. You must move forward, leave the past behind you and focus on healing!

> *"Bear with each other and forgive one another if any of you has a grievance against someone. Forgive as the Lord forgave you."*
> Colossians 3:13

- **Accept your family members for who they are.**

    You will never be able to change your family, so learn to accept them for who they are. The loud auntie, the overly religious grandma, the "mack daddy" uncle and the "to cool for school" cousins----love them all!

    "Accept other believers who are weak in faith, and don't argue with them about what they think is right or wrong."
    Romans 14:1 NLT

I'm sure you may have your own personal family drama. You might even dread the holidays because all the family members you despise will be there. That's perfectly normal. You are not alone. The fact remains that they are still your family despite all they put you through. I know you love your family, but you must also know when to separate yourself in order to grow into the person that you are meant to become. Continue to keep them covered in prayer as God leads them in their individual lives.

CHAPTER EIGHT

FRIENDS OR "FRENEMIES"

Serious question: "Am I the only one who feels like they don't have any friends?"

As popular as I was in high school, I always felt disconnected from everyone. Since 2012, I've bounced from career to career, surrounded by successful people who the average person would love to establish friendships with. I always struggled with building relationships with my coworkers because I couldn't find a genuine connection. When I was teaching, it seemed like every moment the teachers weren't in the classroom or planning their lessons, they wanted to drink the agony of being surrounded by mouthy and disruptive children away. They invited me to happy hour hangouts, but I couldn't muster the desire to go. I was uninterested for two reasons: I didn't drink, and we didn't have anything in common except the fact that we were teachers. I was missing the connection and even though people gravitated to my positive, energetic disposition, I was really a loner on the inside.

After feeling frustrated about my inability to make friends, not associates or people that just like to hang around me, I began to talk to God. I wanted to know why he made me so different and why it was so hard for me to make friends. I started to analyze the people around me. Most of them didn't align with who I was or where I wanted to be; non-believers, party-girls, people with sexual desires that didn't align with mine and the ever-present leeches. When your friends don't align with your greater purpose in life, God will cause those relationships to feel broken and draining. As God began to do a work in me spiritually, I separated myself from those friends that I didn't foresee helping me to grow as a Christian. As a result, people thought I was bourgeois and "standoffish". They called me mean and rude. You name it. I explained my spiritual journey to them, but they didn't want to accept it. So, I had to remove them from my life because God meant more to me than our friendships.

I had too many friends that were using and abusing me while leading me closer to the enemy, instead of on the path of righteousness. I call them "frenemies." One "frenemy" would encourage me to go clubbing with her because she knew my beauty would attract good-looking men. Another "frenemy" would try to get me drunk so she could entice me sexually. There was the "frenemy" who always called me for advice and counseling but never called to check on me when I was going through my divorce. I also had a "frenemy" who loved to evoke doubt in me by infecting me with their pessimistic thoughts and feelings. No matter how positive I was, she always found something negative to counter it with. Like a desert, I was dried out, drained of every drop of living water I had.

I'm sure you have some "frenemies" in your life. Hypocrites are friends that never show up to support you but will curse you out and call you "disloyal" if you don't support them. Manipulating friends will always want to go out, but never have money, so you constantly pay the bill. Then later you see them post a picture on Facebook of their new $500 weave. Superficial friends will talk about you, stab you in your back, but then smile in your face. Envious friends hate to see you win, but love to watch you fail. Sabotaging friends won't walk with you on your spiritual journey; they'll fight against it. If you want a life of freedom you must immediately get rid of these want-to-be, envy-filled, fake behind friends. They don't deserve your friendship and you don't need theirs.

God made human beings to be relational, which means we are meant to have relationships, communicate and interact with other human beings. We determine whether those relationships are good or bad by the people we choose to develop relationships with. So, when I made the decision to move on from my "frenemies", God allowed new friends to enter my life. At 23, I joined Enon Tabernacle Baptist Church and began fellowshipping with the Ignite Young Adult Ministry. I was surrounded by Christians my age who were genuinely trying to live a life of Christ. Two people, Jason and Crystal, helped open my eyes to true friendship. They would call to check on me, pray with me, invite me to game nights and fellowships as well as challenge me when I wasn't putting God first in my life. I always felt a genuine connection because they both truly had a heart for God. Every friendship I developed since then had to have this same essence. Despite me leaving Enon in 2016 to attend Epic Church, our friendship still remains the same. I am now fortunate enough to have good friends, from both churches, who love and challenge me to be a better Christian.

You, too, should surround yourself with people who challenge you to live better. Establishing true friendships is a major part of growing as an individual, however, you must determine which friends are real and which ones are "frenemies." Read these tips to determine if you can find some of these qualities in your current friendships.

Dana Marie's 8 Tips for Filtering Friendships

- **A true friend will support you in all your endeavors.**

Sometimes as you discover yourself, you change your mind about how you want your life to go. A true friend will support you when you make the decision to go from selling t-shirts to becoming a pastor. They will always be there to encourage you and provide whatever help they can. Even if they don't fully understand, they will be there.

> *"But Ruth replied, "Don't ask me to leave you and turn back. Wherever you go, I will go; wherever you live, I will live. Your people will be my people, and your God will be my God."*
> Ruth 1:16 NLT

- **A true friend will be forgiving.**

When you and your friend have a fight, you should already count yourself as forgiven because that's what real friends do. This doesn't mean you have a free pass to intentionally hurt one another. That would be insensitive and cruel. It means that if your friend has a heart like Christ than they will most likely forgive you as often as you need it.

> *"Even if that person wrongs you seven times a day and each time turns again and asks forgiveness, you must forgive."*
> Luke 17:4 NLT

- **A true friend will always have your back.**

Jesus was with his friend, Peter, in the garden, when the Roman soldiers came to arrest him, after Judas had sold his whereabouts. As the soldiers went to apprehend Jesus, Peter took out his sword and cut one of their right ears off (See John 18:1-14). Peter wasn't playing any games when it came to Jesus. Just like Peter, a true friend will stand for you and with you no matter what happens. They protect you from hurt and danger. However, don't be surprised if they check you for something stupid you did in private. That's what friends do. They will always be there for you both physically and mentally.

> *"When Job's three friends, Eliphaz the Temanite, Bildad the Shuhite and Zophar the Naamathite, heard about all the troubles that had come upon him, they set out from their homes and met together by agreement to go and sympathize with him and comfort him."*
> Job 2:11

- **A true friend will encourage self-discovery.**

You have the right to learn more about yourself and a real friend should want you to. They won't discourage you from making choices that benefit you. They will walk the path of self-discovery with you as you grow stronger, wiser, smarter and savvier. Good friends will especially encourage you to strengthen your relationship with God. They'll admire your spiritual growth and support you along the way.

> *"As iron sharpens iron, so a friend sharpens a friend."*
> Proverbs 27:17 NLT

- **A true friend will know the real you.**

A real friend pays attention to you; they know your dating preferences, favorite foods, and little quirks. They notice all your interesting characteristics and can give you advice based on their observations. Sometimes you may not even realize your moody because you're hungry and your friend will just show up with snacks. They know you inside out, when you are overacting or being naïve. That's why they are the best advisors when it comes to making the best decisions for you.

> *"An open rebuke is better than hidden love! Wounds from a sincere friend are better than many kisses from an enemy."*
> Proverbs 27:5-6 NLT

- **A true friend can always be trusted.**

    True friends will never talk about you behind your back--- maybe to your face though. These types of friends won't try to sabotage you and your dreams. They won't steal your joy or belittle your ideas. You can trust that they'll pray for you and encourage you to take the right path. They will be there to love you and give you peace of mind.

    > *"A friend is always loyal, and a brother is born to help in time of need."*
    > Proverbs 17:17 NLT

- **A true friend will never judge you.**

    In life, you will make horrible mistakes and your friend will be there to listen to you vent without making you feel insecure and stupid. Your friends never judge you, instead, they will empathize with your pain and provide good advice. Your deepest, darkest secrets are safe in your friend's hands. You can do the ugly face, snotty nose cry, without any judgment!

    > *"And why worry about a speck in your friend's eye when you have a log in your own?"*
    > Matthew 7:3 NLT

- **A true friend will make time for you.**

    Even when marriage, work, school and LIFE begins to occupy their time (making your friends unavailable and unreachable) they won't allow it to interrupt the relationship. No matter how busy or how far you are apart, a true friend will make you a priority in their life. They will call, visit when money and time permits and maybe even send letters or gifts. They remember birthdays and important dates in your life because they genuinely care for you.

> *"There are "friends" who destroy each other,*
> *but a real friend sticks closer than a brother."*
> Proverbs 18:24 NLT

The power of friendship can bring you down or lift you up. I urge you to choose your friends wisely and don't be afraid to cut some people off. If they aren't helping to make your life better, then toss them to the curb. No fake friends, no fake love, and no fake support! True friendship is everlasting. True friendship is consistent and true friendship is needed. Now go assess your friends!

CHAPTER NINE

AGAPE LOVE

In 2012, after my divorce, I decided it was time to give love another chance. I went full fledge into another relationship that was just as bad, if not worse, than my marriage. I was so distraught over my divorce as well as so adamant about my child growing up with a father (because I didn't) that I was desperate to be in another relationship without taking the time to completely heal. Listen to this mess...

A well-known Philadelphia musician was having a huge end of the summer pool party and my sister encouraged me to go. We waited in frustration as the line wrapped around the corner of the privately-owned pool club in Northern Liberties. While we were waiting in line, one of the bass players walked by us, heading to the front. My sister screamed out to him with a high-pitched voice in hopes of gaining some sympathy and expedited entry. He fell for it and let us walk in by his side, jumping ahead of the hundreds of people waiting in line. The music blasting from the speakers radiated down my legs. I sat at the table with my arms folded looking at all the half-naked women and fully clothed men walking in.

As I began to bob my head, a familiar face energetically started dancing toward me. I couldn't help but smile. Firstly, because it was the dumbest dance I'd even seen, and secondly, because I hadn't seen that face since middle school. The party turned into our own private oasis as we tuned out the music and tuned into each other. We talked the whole night, reminiscing about our friendship, annoying teachers and old-school musicals. He told me about his career as a musician and what God was doing in his life. I told him about my divorce and God's vision for my future. We didn't skip a beat, just that quick we were best friends again.

The conversations didn't stop that night, day after day, we'd talk on the phone about how he used to be so madly in love with me. I'd chuckled a little, but was still reserved about opening my heart to him. I used to tell myself I would never date a musician because of the stereotypes associated with the profession. They were labeled as leeches, whores, and drug addicts. Although I had this inkling about musicians, I believed he was different and wanted to give him a chance. We got serious pretty fast. Within three months I let him meet my two-year-old daughter. They instantly formed the father-daughter connection that I longed for as a child. He'd pick her up and twirl her around in the air and teach her phrases like "please" and "thank you". He showed her the different notes on his keyboard while he sang the ABC song. It was the sweetest thing to watch. I knew deep down inside that I was rushing getting into another relationship, but I adored how he was such a great father figure to my daughter. I decided to let him move in with us for the family to be complete. What I didn't know is that was all a part of the game, finding an established, yet battered woman to financially support them as they pursue their dreams. Meanwhile manipulating, using and abusing them to continuously get what they need. Even if it meant using my child as the pawn.

Months went by and all the lies he told about being a successful musician and touring began to surface. He wasn't touring and wasn't making any money at all. He smoked and drank way more than he'd indicated when we first started dating. When I questioned him about it he made promises to slow down but never did. The motivation to succeed dwindled, as he sat in the house all day gossiping about how fake all the other musicians were. I found myself taking care of two people, my child, and this grown man. I was giving him money, supporting his dream, cooking, cleaning, paying bills while he worked late nights in the studio.

When he was touring and making money again his ego swelled so big that his respect and appreciation for me all disappeared. What used to be soft whispers of love became piercing screams of hate. He would bring up my marriage and how I was molested as a child. This man even began to have a problem with my child, saying he hated the fact that I was a mom. I remember one time, he was so disgusted with me for being a divorced single mother that he choked me so hard I almost lost my life. The verbal and mental abuse was more than enough, but physical abuse was the final straw. I knew I had to leave because he put his hands on me. Oddly though, there were still moments I wanted to stay because of the relationship he had with my daughter. Tangled between the two decisions, I finally gave up on my relationship after almost three years.

It was 2015 when I left him. I was so devastated at how unapologetic he was for hurting me. My heart was shattered into pieces and my stomach felt too sick to swallow any food. I hated myself for keeping him a part of our lives for so long when I knew he wasn't truly vested in us. This man used up my money, lived in my house, ran up my credit and lied to me about wanting to be a father to my daughter. I was like a lemon rotting in the sun, bitter and heated.

I felt the Lord nudging at me, trying to get my attention. I heard him say, "Dana you've allowed this man to steal all my attention for too long distracting you from recognizing the love I have for you. Come back to me I will give you rest."

For the millionth time in my life, I ran back to God. Falling to my knees, I prayed for forgiveness and healing. I began to read scriptures in the Bible specifically about love, agape love. That's when I realized that I'd never experienced true love, but I knew I wanted to and that I deserved it. I began to patiently wait for God to send me someone who would love me correctly, and because of my faithfulness and dedication to him, he did.

In July 2016, I met an amazing man named Warren. It was true friendship at first sight. The authentic connection between us sparked like a firework on the fourth of July as we talked all night about life and God. We realized at that moment we weren't ready to be together as a couple because we both were in the process of healing our mind, body, and spirit. Still, we didn't go too far apart. We went to see Kevin Hart's movie, "What Now?" and had the time of our lives. Laughter filled the air and joy melted our hearts. We knew at that moment it was time to at least try to move forward with each other.

We developed a closer relationship by allowing God to serve as the center of attention between us. I saw how sincere he was about his future with me and how honest he was about his weaknesses. This transparency left no room for doubt in our relationship. He continued listening attentively to all my worries and one by one casts them on the Lord. To this day, he faithfully lifts me up, supports my dream and prays me through. Our desire to keep God first, make daily sacrifices for each other and love unconditionally is what makes our relationship successful. Even when times get rough we can stand firm on the word believing that love never gives up, never loses faith, is always hopeful, and endures through every circumstance. (See 1 Corinthians 13:7) We are the epitome of black, agape love ordained by God. In Fall 2018, we will finally make our union one before friends, family and most importantly God.

> "But at the beginning of creation, God 'made them male and female.' For this reason, a man will leave his father and mother and be united to his wife, and the two will become one flesh. So they are no longer two, but one flesh. Therefore, what God has joined together, let no one separate."
> Mark 10:6-9

Since discovering the truth about what love is, how to love and why it's important I want you to learn the same. I realized that in the Christian community we use the term "agape love" loosely without fully recognizing its power. Agape love is love in its highest form, comparable to the unconditional, sacrificial love God has for his people. God loved the word so much that he sent his only son to die on the cross for us to be saved. (See John 3:16) Now that's love! My goal is that, if you desire, you will receive true, agape love like I have. In 2014 only 29% of African Americans were married compared to 48% of all Americans. Half or 50% of African Americans have never been married compared to 33% of all Americans (Black Demographics). When we as a people achieve that right type of love, agape love, we will see these statistics change.

I promise it's one of the best feelings in the world to have someone by your side, loving you the same way Jesus does. No matter what phase you are in from single to dating to already married use these tips to help you understand and recognize agape love.

Dana Marie's 8 Tips for Understanding Agape Love

- **Agape love is love at its highest, purest form.**

    This love is the epitome of God. To love is to know God. As you and your mate began to spend more time with God, read his word, meditate, pray and grow spiritually, you both will learn how to love one another the way God loves us.

    > *"Whoever does not love does not know God,
    > because God is love."*
    > 1 John 4:8

- **Agape love is sacrificial!**

    You and your mate must be willing to lay down your strongest desires to satisfy the needs and desires of one another. Before you make a selfish decision, consider the feelings and needs of your mate, which ultimately ends in a sacrifice. There are no conditions on this type of love; it's love that is unconditional. So, no matter what the sacrifice is you must be willing, through love, to make the change.

    > *"This is how we know what love is: Jesus Christ
    > laid down his life for us. And we ought to lay down our
    > lives for our brothers and sisters."*
    > 1 John 3:16

- **Agape love is never harmful.**

    Don't ever believe that the ABUSIVE, whether it's physically, mentally or emotionally, man or woman you are in a relationship with truly loves you. Agape love will always keep you safe and protected from intentional hurts and wrongdoings. There won't be grudges, verbal abuse, domestic abuse, discouragement and emptiness with this type of love.

> *"Love does no harm to a neighbor.*
> *Therefore it is a fulfillment of the law."*
> Romans 13:10

- **Agape love is patient, kind and true.**

This love allows you to grow into the person you are supposed to be while your mate willingly waits for your transformation to occur. You will never have to worry about dishonesty because in the word we know that the truth is Jesus and Jesus is love, so any man that's in Christ is in love. There is patience with love, so as you get yourself together, your mate should be there praying and encouraging you all the way.

> *"So Jacob worked seven years to pay for Rachel.*
> *But his love for her was so strong that it seemed*
> *to him but a few days."*
> Genesis 29:20 NLT

- **Agape love is always reciprocal.**

Picture your mate constantly speaking life into you, whispering "sweet somethings" in your ear and making you feel like a 6-year-old with a crush. The person you decide to spend any part of your life with whether 6 months or sixty years, should receive the same agape love you expect to receive from them. You are entitled to being loved at the highest level and so is your mate. Just like God desires you to love him back, you should expect your mate to do the same.

> *"We love because he first loved us."*
> 1 John 4:19

- **Agape love is expressed through action.**

A person who loves you will show you by being patient, kind, truthful, selfless, forgiving, encouraging, and sacrificial. When people show you who they are, believe them. When they show you hatred, disrespect, and discouragement they mean it. Get out and get out fast because they don't know how to love. Determine if you're just wasting precious time with someone who doesn't even have the capacity to show you how to live a fuller, richer life.

> *"Dear children, let's not merely say that we love each other; let us show the truth by our actions."*
> 1 John 3:18 NLT

- **Agape love is a lasting partnership.**

A partnership is an agreement formed between two people who both want to benefit from the agreement. You should desire to grow with, build with and learn from your partner. Before solidifying your relationship think of the benefits you could receive from being with this person as well as what you have to offer. Will he or she motivate you, help to keep you organized, provide financial assistance or emotional support? Your spouse is supposed to be a helpmate, just as Eve was to Adam in the Garden of Eden (See Genesis 2:18). Next, think about ways in which both of you can partner together to spread the love and gospel of Jesus Christ.

> *"Two people are better off than one, for they can help each other succeed. If one person falls, the other can reach out and help. But someone who falls alone is in real trouble."*
> Ecclesiastes 4:9-10 NLT

- **Agape love is forgiving!**

You shouldn't be ridiculed because of your past, nor should you do that to your mate. Jesus has forgiven us a multitude of times as well as given us grace and mercy. We must show this same love, grace, and mercy. You can love someone and forgive him or her, but you don't necessarily have to reconcile the relationship. There are some situations as in domestic violence, in which you may want to forgive and keep it moving. You don't deserve someone beating on you, stealing from you, lying to you and manipulating you, however, you still must forgive. Forgiveness is a key component of love!

> *"I will make you my wife forever, showing you righteousness and justice, unfailing love and compassion."*
> Hosea 2:19 NLT

If by chance you are having difficulties finding and experiencing agape love, continue to have faith and trust in God. Don't get weary in well-doing, for in due time you will receive all that God has for you. Society makes periods of singleness seem taboo, but their purpose is to help you develop who you are as an individual. Be single with a purpose. Learn to use your singleness as a tool to develop a standard for when you are in togetherness.

If you are currently in a relationship, ask yourself if you're receiving agape love. Then ask yourself if you're giving agape love. If not, you must be the change you want to see. No man wants to come home to a quarrelsome wife, just like no woman wants a lazy, remote hogging, husband. Take a deeper look at yourself because you may be the problem. Agape love is the best gift you could ever give and the best gift you will ever receive!

Financial Freedom

CHAPTER TEN

BUDGETING: THE MASTER PLAN

When I landed my first full-time, well-paying job I thought I was killing the game. I was working at Target as an Executive Team Leader, making $50,000 a year at 21 years old with very small responsibilities. Long live the red and khaki. My first few checks I went a little crazy traveling, buying clothes and toys for my daughter. My plan was to pay off roughly $10,000 in student loan debt and save $3000 to get an apartment of my own because momma's house wasn't cutting it anymore. I did stick to my plan and by 2013 I was debt free from student loans and moving into my first luxury apartment with a pool and fitness center. Can you say, baller???

Although, sticking to my plan is commendable, when I really think about it, my plan wasn't as thorough as it should have been. After paying debt and saving for my apartment, I had a lot of money left over. As I consider my financial decisions such as eating out excessively, loaning money, buying senseless things just because and splurging on pricey vacations, I realize that I was greedily spending. I was trying to acquire more material things to make me happier with my life and myself. I had the money to do so, so I spent it on more and more things, more and more experiences only to feel more and more dissatisfied. Spending money became my obsession. Sometimes, I look back and say things like, "If only I hadn't bought that $1500 TV, I would have more money in the bank." As I got older, I realized that I needed to get a better control over my financial life. I needed to create an efficient plan and execute it.

There are two factors that determine how you manage your money; fear and greed. In fearful money management, you typically don't take any financial risks and your friends may call you a "cheapskate." Most fearful people never give back via monetary donations, rarely possess or enjoy the finer things in life, and most likely hoard their money. In the Bible, there's the parable of the three servants in Matthew 25:14-30. We learn that there were three servants who were given money by their master, two servants invested it and made a profit. The third servant buried his money in the ground. When the master came back he was pleased with the two that invested but displeased with the servant who buried it in the ground. The servant said, "I was afraid I would lose your money, so I hid it in the earth. Look, here is your money back." (Matthew 25:25 NLT) Due to fear, the servant was unable to make the best financial decision.

Greedy money management is when you never look at price tags, purchase things just to keep up with the Kardashians and barely have any savings. Greed is an obsession with acquiring material things. God warns us to be careful not to fall into the greed trap of making life about acquiring more things. (See Luke 12:15) When you become more focused on making money to spend it on material things you begin to idolize money. In 1 Timothy 6:10 it says, *"For the love of money is a root of all kinds of evil. Some people, eager for money, have wandered from the faith and pierced themselves with many griefs."* When greed is a factor, your financial decisions are now plagued by evil motives therefore always causing you to spend and mismanage money.

God's plan is for us to be ethical stewards or managers of our finances, after all, he is the one who gives us the ability to make money. (See Deuteronomy 8:17-18) Don't get me wrong, both fear and greed can have positive effects on your financial decisions. For instance, if you fear being old and broke it may encourage you to save more of your money for retirement. The same goes with greed, if you are acquiring more investments or finding newer ways to create more revenue to help build generational wealth for your family than more is great.

I was utilizing both fear and greed when managing my money. My greed caused me to buy material things like a bigger TV when I already had one. I was fearful to invest and even pay my tithes, which God required of me. Tithing is a bible principle where you give 10% of the money you earn back to God so that the church can continue to do the work of Christ.

> *"Bring the whole tithe into the storehouse,*
> *that there may be food in my house. Test me in this,"*
> *says the LORD Almighty, "and see if I will not throw*
> *open the floodgates of heaven and pour out so much blessing*
> *that there will not be room enough to store it."*
> Malachi 3:10

As a Christian tithing should have been in my plan, but fear and greed prevented me from doing so. Without God I wouldn't even be able to make money, so why not break him off with his cut. So, I did by adding tithing to my plan. From this point on I am a faithful tither who trusts God's financial plan for my life.

Establishing control over your finances is one of the most rewarding things you will ever do in life. Money has the ability to ruin marriages, mess up good friendships and stop you from pursuing your dreams. It's your job to take control over your life through control over your money. I'm sure you have a personal goal of financial freedom and it's not a hard task to accomplish if you put your mind to it.

Many Christians living below the poverty line misinterpret the scripture 1 Timothy 6:10 and think money is the root of all. However, God says, *"the love of money is the root of all evil."* I myself am guilty of thinking the same thing. I didn't desire to gain riches because I thought it would lead me further from God. I subconsciously sabotaged my opportunities to be placed in a life-changing economic status because of my views about money. Through research, prayer and bible study I realized I had it all wrong. The more you have the more you give.

The very first step to financial freedom is changing your mindset from poor to wealthy. You must start thinking like wealthy people think. Most wealthy people believe they deserve wealth and have optimistic views about money. They believe in taking financial risk as well as following a strategic plan to help them gain more wealth. If you desire to have financial abundance start examining your spending habits, your credit score, ways to cut cost and financial goals. Your mindset shift will cause you to create a well-rounded budget, a plan for how you will spend your money, which ultimately keeps you on track to financial freedom. When you don't have a plan for your money you will most likely make bad financial decisions, so here are some tips to becoming a good steward of your money.

Dana Marie's Tips for Brilliant Budgeting

- **Create a WRITTEN monthly budget.**

    Writing is the most important part of this tip because it creates a tangible plan that you can refer to. Your budget should include ALL your income: money coming in from work, selling products/services, child support, etc. as well as all your expenses: money going out for mortgage, insurance, car loans, credit cards, donations, vacations etc. Don't forget to write it down. If you actually see the vision, you will most likely execute more effectively.

    > *"The plans of the diligent lead to profit as surely as haste leads to poverty."*
    > Proverbs 21:5

- **Determine whether each item on your budget is a NECESSITY or LUXURY.**

    Necessities are things like food and rent. Luxuries are things like movie dates and shopping sprees. If you start eliminating some of the luxury expenses you will have more money to get you out of debt and build your savings.

    > *"After all, we brought nothing with us when we came into the world, and we can't take anything with us when we leave it. So if we have enough food and clothing, let us be content."*
    > 1 Timothy 6:7-8 NLT

- **Find savvy ways to save money on things you use/buy every day.**

    The first way to save is by conserving energy and water. Simple things like turning off the water while brushing your teeth and turn off/down your heat when you're not home and even canceling subscriptions you don't use often such as, (Netflix, gym memberships, Spotify etc.) You can also search for coupons to save money on groceries and other household items. Being wasteful whether with food or electricity can cause deep holes in your pockets.

> *"When they had all had enough to eat,*
> *he said to his disciples, "Gather the pieces that*
> *are left over. Let nothing be wasted."*
> John 6:12

- **Budget with your family.**

God wants us to be good stewards of our money. Sometimes it's hard to stay on track when everyone else is pressuring you to deviate from the budget. That's why talking to your family about the budget will help everyone get on the same page. This will help foster financial literacy in your family as well as provide accountability partners. You are also teaching your children how to be good stewards of their finances, which fosters their ability to make better financial decisions in adulthood.

> *"Direct your children onto the right path,*
> *and when they are older, they will not leave it."*
> Proverbs 22:6 NLT

- **Understand that you will mess up your budget.**

Life happens! You might have an expected medical emergency, expensive home repair or even more college fees than expected that need to get paid. Better yet you might just splurge on that Bahamian vacation or those Louboutin shoes. It's ok, you made a mistake. Don't beat yourself up, just remember your goal to be financially free, and then get back on track. It's never too late to start over and you're never too far to go back. Like Nike, just do it! Your dream of financial freedom can still come true.

> *"We want each of you to show this same diligence to the very end, so that what you hope for may be fully realized."*
> Hebrews 6:11

- **Establish an Emergency Fund.**

  Like I said before, life happens. That's why you must have an emergency fund, the money you save for emergencies and unexpected expenses, so you won't mess up your budget. This fund provides a safety net for you. Random financial obligations will come up out of the blue, so if you're prepared to handle it you won't have a budget set back. God wants you to be safe, not sorry, because he already foresees the issues you'll face in this world.

  > *"Invest in seven ventures, yes, in eight; you do not know what disaster may come upon the land."*
  > Ecclesiastes 11:2

- **Reevaluate and adjust your budget as needed.**

Ok, so you got promoted, congratulations. Now you must create a new budget because you have more money coming in that doesn't have a purpose. Or let's say you have a new car loan, the old, rusty, worn down car just wasn't doing its job anymore. Well, guess what, you must add the car payments and insurance to your budget. Money that you used to spend on recreation may now have to go to the car payments. The main key is to be sure to "write out" the new budget and get your family on board. Your budget will most likely change at some point in your life.

> *"It was like this for the twenty years I was in your household. I worked for you fourteen years for your two daughters and six years for your flocks, and you changed my wages ten times."*
> Genesis 31:41

- **Most importantly remember to always pay yourself.** People think paying yourself means shopping sprees and extravagant vacations. However, paying yourself really means setting aside a portion of your money to establish a secure financial future. In layman's terms, it's simply saving money! You must include saving in your budget and stick to it. If you want a secure financial future, saving is one way to receive it.

"On the first day of every week, each one of you should set aside a sum of money in keeping with your income, saving it up, so that when I come no collections will have to be made."
1 Corinthians 16:2

As you prepare your budget make sure you include the most important part, tithing. If you're someone who is already struggling to pay your bills I know tithing may seem impossible, but I urge you to trust God. Trust that God will bless you exceedingly and abundantly because of your faithfulness to him. Don't allow fear to stop you from giving what you owe to God. Activate your faith and watch God bless you financially.

CHAPTER ELEVEN

THE LIFE SAVER

In January 2013, I was blessed with the opportunity to move to Connecticut to be a part of the Fast Track Management Program with Save-A-Lot. I was making over $50,000 per year and was on target to reaching six figures as a District Manager. However, in May I was faced with a harsh reality, no reliable babysitter. I couldn't bear to leave my daughter, Jaisa, at home in Philadelphia so I brought her along to Connecticut, but the long, inconsistent hours that retail provided left me no hope for finding a reliable, trustworthy sitter. There's this thing in retail called a "Clopen." It's when you close the store, typically at midnight, and reopen at about 6 am. "Clopens" were my life and after a while, it became harder to find someone to match my inconsistent work hours. I can honestly say that having a savings made it easier to make the decision to return home.

I left Save-A-Lot in May to come back home where my support system was. I had $6000 saved in my emergency fund. Desperate to move, I used that money for moving expenses back to Pennsylvania and a security deposit on my new house in Southwest Philadelphia. When I got back to Philly I had no plan, no job and only $3000 left to last until I figured something out. I'd wake up in cold sweats from panicking as I watched my savings deplete day to day. Fear grew in my heart, as I wondered how long I'd have to depend on the welfare system to put food in my refrigerator. My fingers bled from the countless hours of typing my resume into the online applications, hoping to find one that would give me some type of financial security. Agony filled my spirit and my faith began wavering like Peter walking on the water to Jesus. Prayer was my only option because I'd literally done all I could do.

After a few weeks, I looked at my savings and saw $.77 cents, with rent due and a car note. I was hopeless. Then, the phone rang as I was wiping the tears from my face.

"Hello!" I said sniffling.

"Is this Dana Randolph?" said the mysterious voice on the phone.

"Yes, who's calling?"

At that moment my voice shifted from sad, soft sobs to a deep, disguising tone because I had no idea who it was.

"This is Piedmont calling to let you know we received your online application and would like to schedule an interview."

My spirit literally left my body as I continued to sit at the table holding the phone. God had seen my diligence in applying for jobs. He saw that I needed his help with only $.77 left. I was grateful that I had a savings account that helped sustain me through this financial drought. I replenished my savings account ready to tackle whatever else came my way financially.

Little did I know that in less than nine months I'd be forced to move again. The house in Southwest Philadelphia was being sold by the owners and in my lease, which I didn't thoroughly read out of desperation to move to back to Philly so quickly, stated that I'd have to vacant in 30 days if they sold the house. I only had about $2000 in my savings. Luckily, I was able to find an apartment in the Mount Airy section of Philadelphia two weeks later. If you're from Philly, then you know Mount Airy is considered "uptown" where all the high society, upscale bourgeois people live. Compared to where I used to live, the crime rates and drug trafficking was significantly lower. Although I was overwhelmed with moving again, I was excited that my daughter had an opportunity to attend a better school in Mount Airy. I used $1300 for a security deposit and $250 for moving expenses. Once again, my savings account saved my life. Life was great, a job, a house and still a few bucks saved in the bank.

Things were going well for some time, but about a year later, I walked up to the white door of my Mount Airy apartment to find an oversized eviction notice hammered in the center. I snatched the note from the door, scanning it from left to right, up and down to figure out what, why and how. I paid my rent on time, so I couldn't understand why I was being evicted. I ran upstairs to the second floor where my landlord stayed. The apartment was as empty as a black hole. I tried dialing his number, back to back, like an obsessed ex-girlfriend not ready to end the relationship, but still no answer. I banged on one of the tenant's doors and she answered with bloodshot red eyes. She was getting evicted, too. I stepped inside to talk to her and help since she was already packing her things. She told me that the guy who'd been collecting rent and claiming to be the manager of the property was lying this whole time. The building had been in foreclosure years before I got there, but this lying slumlord didn't tell anyone the property was in foreclosure. He falsely collected rent and security deposits scamming innocent tenants out of their money.

    I lost my security deposit and was forced to move again. This time I didn't have enough money to move into another apartment. I was trying to aggressively tackle my credit card debt, so I barely saved this time. Thankfully, I had a mother who allowed my daughter and I to live with her until we got enough money to move again. The financial and emotional stress of moving so many times made me realize how important it is to save money. Can you imagine if I didn't have the money to move each time? I would have been homeless or living in an overcrowded house with relatives.

    If you've ever ventured off and had your own place, then you know that going back home is humbling. You can't live by your rules because you're no longer the ruler of the house. Even when I moved back home with my mother, I was appreciative, but it was very challenging to go from lots of personal space to no space because everyone else in the household invades your privacy. God had allowed me to work and save money because he knew that life has unexpected challenges. For the most part, having a savings saved my life. Your savings could save yours.

    I don't want to assume you already know what saving is. Here's my definition, saving is the process of setting aside a portion of your current income for the future. You may be saving money for retirement, to buy your dream house, for an emergency fund or even for your child's college tuition. Whatever the case may be, saving money on a monthly basis is very important. If you get into the routine of saving money now it will become a habit later. Don't worry about how much you're saving just start with something. Whether $10 or $1000 a month, the consistency of saving is your main goal. As you get better at saving, you will become more creative by diversifying your savings options, this includes investing. Some investment options include bank products, stocks, bonds, mutual funds, and certificate of deposits. No amount is too small, and consistency is key when saving money. Here are a few tips on how to save money more successfully than you ever have.

Dana Marie's 8 Tips for Saving Successfully

- **Know that your savings serve a purpose.**

  Know the purpose of the money you are saving whether for college, a house, retirement or your dream vacation. There are so many reasons to save money. Sometimes the money you're saving might not even be for you. The Bible talks about the generation wealth and leaving your family an inheritance. So, if you don't have any items to save for than save for your children and their children to come.

  > *"A good person leaves an inheritance for their children's children, but a sinner's wealth is stored up for the righteous."*
  > Proverbs 13:22

- **Save your money automatically.**

  Most people have direct deposit, so have your "budgeted" savings amount directly deposited into a separate, hard to access savings accounts. There are online banks like ING Direct and Ally that will help make saving money easier because you don't have as much excess to it as you would a Wells Fargo or PNC bank. The more difficult it is to take out the money the less likely you will be tempted to touch it. Saving automatically will increase your chances of saving effectively. You should also have a separate emergency fund for future emergencies. However, no matter what account you use the goal is to save money in the bank.

  > *"Why then didn't you put my money on deposit, so that when I came back, I could have collected it with interest?"*
  > Luke 19:23

- **Set up realistic savings goals.**

Listen I'm all for dreamers, but if you set a goal to save $1,000,000 but your work ethic and finances don't line up, you need to reevaluate. Be frank with yourself about how much you can afford to save. It's okay to aim high, but your work ethic must match your savings goal. Be real with yourself so that you won't feel like a failure if you don't reach your goal.

> *"For by the grace given me I say to every one of you:*
> *Do not think of yourself more highly than you ought, but*
> *rather think of yourself with sober judgment, in accordance*
> *with the faith God has distributed to each of you."*
> Romans 12:3

- **Always have a savings plan!**

Write down how much you will save every paycheck/date and how long it will take you to reach your goal. For instance, if your purpose is to purchase a car for $6000, then you will need to save $250 every paycheck twice per month for 12 months to get that $6000. Save with a purposeful plan!

> *"Suppose one of you wants to build a tower.*
> *Won't you first sit down and estimate the cost to see*
> *if you have enough money to complete it? For if you lay*
> *the foundation and are not able to finish it, everyone*
> *who sees it will ridicule you, saying, 'This person*
> *began to build and wasn't able to finish.'"*
> Luke 14:28-30

- **Begin your retirement savings early!**

It's never too soon to save for retirement. If you're employed, start with your job's 401(k) for profit businesses or 403(b) for non-profit businesses. You may also find that your employer offers a Company Match Program in which they match the amount of money you save in your retirement account typically around 3-6%. Only 54.3 percent of African

Americans work for an employer who offers a retirement plan, compared to 62 percent of White workers (Center for Global Policy Solutions). If you're self-employed or don't have a company plan set up an Individual Retirement Account with a bank or credit union to start saving.

> *"This applies to the Levites: Men twenty-five years old or more shall come to take part in the work at the tent of meeting, but at the age of fifty, they must retire from their regular service and work no longer."*
> Numbers 8:24-25

- **Save all your loose change.**

Pennies are money. I repeat PENNIES are MONEY! Get yourself a big jug and start putting your change in the jug. Every time you go to the corner store or pay a toll take that change directly to your change jar. At the end of each year deposit the change into your savings account. This is a simple way to build wealth one penny at a time.

> *"Dishonest money dwindles away, but whoever gathers money little by little makes it grow."*
> Proverbs 13:11

- **Use your tax refunds, settlements, inheritance and any lump sums of money to fuel your savings account.**

If you're expecting some extra cash, and truly don't need it to get you caught up on your bills, live as if it's not coming. This isn't your opportunity to splurge on a shopping spree. If you can afford to save it all, do so. If not, use it wisely, tackle some debt and get ahead on your bills. It will pay off in the long run!

> *"The wise have wealth and luxury, but fools spend whatever they get."*
> Proverbs 21:20 NLT

- **Stay on track as much as possible. If you fall short, get back to the plan.**

    Sometimes it's hard to stay on track because the urges to spend are powerful. Remember what your ultimate goal for saving is. For a house? For generational wealth? For emergencies? Think about how accomplished you'll feel when you reach your goal. If the struggle gets real, of course, pray, but try what I call the "Match Spending Program." When you buy French fries at Checkers put the same amount of money you spent on the fries into your savings account. Trust and believe you will start to cut a lot of unnecessary spending.

    > *"You must not turn aside, for then you would go after futile things which cannot profit or deliver, because they are futile."*
    > 1 Samuel 12:21 NASB

Saving money can save your life in many instances. It can prevent you from being homeless, allow you to tackle unexpected medical expenses, or even provide you with the vacation of your dreams. My desire is for you to be rich with a purpose, but to get there you must start by budgeting and saving the money you have now. God needs to see that you are faithful with the little bit he gives you before the bigger blessings start coming in. After you've developed a habit of saving and budgeting you will start to see a shift in your financial decision-making. Now it's time to tackle all your debt!

CHAPTER TWELVE

SLAVES TO THE LENDER

At 15, I started reading Suze Orman books just because I was so saddened by the black communities' financial ignorance, which ultimately resulted in living in poverty. I remember going to the gas station with one of my white friends who had already had a car. He was at the gas pump and pulled out an American Express credit card with his name on it. His mother allowed him to be an authorized user on her credit card to help him establish good credit habits earlier than the average person. I had no idea what credit or credit cards were. As a kid, I'd see people swiping these flimsy plastic things when it was time to pay for stuff, but I thought it was magic. As I dug a little deeper into finances, reading Suze Orman and the Bible, I learned so much about saving, budgeting, credit, and debt.

The question stands, "Did I apply the knowledge I learned as a teenager about financial management in my adulthood?" The answer is "Ahhhhh… no." I was not as responsible as I should have been with my finances. By the time I was 19 years old I had over $10,000 in student loan debt and two car notes for an Acura and Mercedes Benz because my ex-husband had horrible credit and couldn't get a car loan. I also had over $8000 in credit card debt. Ask me what I bought on those credit cards; it was name brand clothes, shoes, vacations and gifts for people. I knew that I was borrowing this money, but that didn't stop me from going to the mall buying four pairs of $200 Jeffrey Campbell shoes, when I already had enough shoes to wear. The financial decisions I was making didn't coincide with scripture. The bible tells us not to take out loans for other people, especially if you're going to risk your own security. (See Proverbs 17:18) I had to be responsible enough to hustle hard to pay everything back. For God would be displeased if I didn't honor my debts, "It is better that you should not vow than that you should vow and not pay." (See Ecclesiastes 5:5) So, I established a budget, savings goal and debt repayment plan. Little by little, I began to pay each debtor off, until they vanished like a thief in the night.

In 2017, The Federal Reserve Bank of New York issued its Quarterly Report on Household Debt and Credit, which reported that total household debt reached $12.73 trillion in the first quarter of 2017 and finally surpassed its $12.68 trillion peak reached during the recession in 2008 (Federal Reserve Bank). You, my friend, are most likely contributing to that huge number of consumer debt. I'm sorry to be the bearer of bad news, but you will never be financially free as long as you are a borrower. In Proverbs 22:7 it states that *"the rich rule over the poor, and the borrower is a slave to the lender."* This simply means that if you owe someone else money, you are supposed to do whatever it takes, work, sweat, toil, until the debt is repaid. Some of you are slaves to student loans borrowed to help pay for education and school-related expenses. You might have a mortgage, money borrowed to pay for a house. Then there's credit cards, car loans, personal loans and small business loans. These loans must be paid back to the people or companies you borrowed from.

Most people borrow money to buy things they don't have enough cash on demand to pay for. If you're like me that's when you depend on credit to make it happen for you. Essentially, you are borrowing money or resources from another person/company to be paid back, later, with interest (additional cost accrued for the duration of the loan that must be paid along with the original loan amount). We've adopted this idea that instant satisfaction beats delayed gratification, so we become unwilling to save, over time, for anything that can be bought right away. If you don't have it in cash you put it on a credit card or take out a loan, right? Well, if it's for that house you want for your family, of course, a loan is great, but your material desires can wait.

Can you imagine living without any bills? Without having to pay back any loans? Close your eyes and imagine what that looks like. All the money you make will go directly to you, not some company overcharging you interest to borrow money. Your desire should be to earn interest, not pay it. The goal is for you to eliminate all your debt as quickly as possible. It's true when they say time is money because the longer you're in debt the more you must pay in interest.

It saddens me when I see more and more people, especially blacks, in such financial holes. They borrow money, at super high-interest rates, mainly because they have a low credit score. A credit score is a number from 300-850 that's used by lenders to determine how much of a financial risk you'd be and your individual creditworthiness. In 2013, more than 64 percent of white American borrowers had a FICO score of 720 or higher compared with 41 percent of Latino borrowers and 33 percent of African-American borrowers (Holmes). The higher your score the lower your risk and the less you'll pay in interest. Sometimes a higher interest rate can double or even triple the amount you have to pay back, so it's important to establish good credit habits like paying your bills on time, utilizing less than 20% of your combined credit card limits and decreasing the frequency of new loan applications. You will have a higher credit score, which essentially means lower interest rates. Your goal should be to borrow less for less. I challenge you to demolish the debt you have and here are some tips to do just that.

Dana Marie's Tips for Destroying Debt

- **Organize all your debt.**

  Make a list of everything you owe from credit cards to personal loans to unpaid medical bills, etc. It is possible to forget about some of the debts you have if you don't make a conscious decision to organize and prioritize.

  > *"Be sure you know the condition of your flocks,*
  > *give careful attention to your herds."*
  > Proverbs 27:23

- **Find quick ways to pay off your debt.**

  Sometimes it's difficult to squeeze extra money out your budget, so extra cash is always a blessing. You may find that you have old clothes you haven't worn since the 90's buried deep down in the closet. Take the things you already have and turn them into profit. Use eBay, Amazon or Craigslist to begin selling what you don't use at a reasonable price to bring in more money for repaying debt. You'll be surprised what people will actually buy.

  > *"She went and told the man of God, and he said,*
  > *"Go, sell the oil and pay your debts. You and your*
  > *sons can live on what is left."*
  > 2 Kings 4:7

- **Consolidate your revolving accounts and refinance your installment loans.**

  Credit cards are considered revolving accounts that allows you to borrow a certain amount of money, up to your credit limit, every month. The purchases you make using your credit card are subject to be charged interest according to the rate listed on your credit card bill. Compare each interest rate and request to have all your credit card balances switched to the card with the lowest interest rate. This process is called a balance transfer, which allows you to manage your debt in one place at a lower cost. Installment loans are loans that you must pay in installments like a mortgage, car note, or personal loan. Search for lower interest rates with other loan companies to see if you can switch your installment loan to their company. This process is called refinancing. Although consumers will check your credit, slightly lowering your credit score, it's worth the money you'll potentially save by refinancing. God didn't intend for you to be charged outrageous interest.

> *"Do not take usurious interest from him, but revere your God, that your countryman may live with you."*
> Leviticus 25:36 (NASB)

- **Pay on time and more than the minimum payment, if possible.**

Review your budget and find out where you can adjust it to increase your debt payments. The more you pay, the faster you will get out of debt and the less money you'll pay in interest. The goal, however, is to at least pay the minimum, because that's what is required of you.

> *"Let no debt remain outstanding, except the continuing debt to love one another, for whoever loves others has fulfilled the law."*
> Romans 13:8

- **Utilize a debt management company.**

A debt management program is typically a nonprofit organization that helps you manage your debt through credit counseling. During this credit counseling, you learn how to increase your fico score, create a plan for debt repayment and establish good financial principles. You do not have to pay a large fee up front to use these companies as you would a Debt Settlement Company. Debt Management programs like the

NFCC and AICCCA are here to help you get back on track financially.

> *"The way of fools seems right to them,*
> *but the wise listen to advice."*
> Proverbs 12:15

- **Avoid debt settlement companies.**

Debt settlement companies make you pay them a LARGE fee up front, as well as a small monthly fee, on top of your designated credit card payment. They call the credit card companies to settle the debt for you. I don't mean to knock the hustle, but you can do that yourself! You could use that extra money to pay more of your debt instead of paying the debt settlement companies. You have no money to waste when debt repayment is your goal.

> *"The prudent see danger and take refuge,*
> *but the simple keep going and pay the penalty."*
> Proverbs 27:12

- **Stick to your debt repayment plan.**

When you get the urge to splurge remember that you are a slave to the borrower. The extra money you receive, use it to pay down more of your debt. The quicker you pay your debt the sooner you become financially free! You will get overwhelmed and feel like giving up, especially when you don't see the results of your labor, but keep the faith.

> *"Let us not become weary in doing good, for at the*
> *proper time we will reap a harvest if we do not give up."*
> Galatians 6:9

- **Stop taking money advice from your broke, full of debt friends and family.**

    Have you had that one friend who always trying to get you to "turn up and live life," spending $300-$400 on bottle service, calling you "cheap" and "frugal" because you're saving or trying to get out of debt, but then need to borrow money to pay their rent? What in the world? First, they try to peer pressure you, then insult you, now they need you to loan them some money. Learn how to say no when they suggest ways for you to get yourself into more debt. Be an advocate for other people in your life, lead them to financial freedom! If you don't teach them, who will?

    "He also told them this parable: "Can the blind lead the blind? Will they not both fall into a pit?"
    Luke 6:39

Now, these are just some of the basics of debt management. Everything I shared with you has literally worked for me. I made a conscious decision to get out of debt when I was 21, I did reach my goal, but of course, I relapsed. I had accumulated debt, splurging at the mall (on other people) and vacationing. When the bills started rolling in the debts started piling up I knew it was time to get back to financial freedom mode. If you don't have the cash, discipline yourself enough to wait.

It can be hard trying to make the best financial decisions, that's why it's important to know what your financial goal is. If you want to be debt free than more of your money will go to repaying debt. If you want to save aggressively to buy a house than more of your money will go into saving. There needs to be a balance in your finances, consisting of saving money, repaying debt and enjoying the fruits of your labor. Know your financial limits and your financial goal, which is to be financially free.

Career Freedom

CHAPTER THIRTEEN

DO WHAT YOU LOVE

There was a point in my life when I went from job to job to job. I literally worked in education, retail, TV, government, entertainment, nonprofit, human resources, fast food, aviation, banking and hair industries over the course of my 27 years of life. I had a one or two-year time span in a field or with one company and then I was gone. I was always in that awkward space where I needed the money and wanted the experience, but I felt out of place. At one job I was the minority, at another my personality was too overwhelming for the office setting. I never felt like I could fit into the small boxes each company tried to put me in. Granted, I'm grateful for the experiences and lessons I learned from each job I've ever had, but I didn't feel like I was walking in my true calling. I learned patience and understanding in the retail industry dealing with irate customers who just wanted to be heard. The entertainment industry taught me hard work and dedication because of all the competition I was up against when auditioning for roles. However, my biggest lesson learned through all my career choices, both, good and bad, was, "Do what you love."

Growing up, I didn't have consistency in my life, my father was a revolving door, my so-called friends only called when they needed me and my faith was always wavering. One day I'd be an insanely holy Christian, the next, a weak, fearful unbeliever. This lack of consistency caused me to hop from one job to the next, following that trend of instability. As I began to pray and ask God to help me with being consistent, he showed me a new revelation. In most cases, I noticed I didn't have a true passion for what I was doing. I'll share something very interesting about me- I hate selling stuff, especially if I think it's crap. I love to give, give and give, so sales and retail were never my passion.

Exuding the phony smile to sell a Target Red Card and persuading clients to open another savings account wasn't my thing. I agonized waking up each morning knowing I was going to a place, to do a job that I had no connection too. I'd wake up, get dressed and go to work at a place that wasn't meant for me. I was spending 8-10 hours making someone else rich and to put the cherry on top, I didn't even like what I was doing, let alone *love* it.

It took a while for me to find out what I truly loved because, in the back of my mind, I loved money. I started chasing jobs based on the dollar amount instead of my passion amount. As began to do some self-discovery I learned what I loved to do most. During the process, my face was buried in the word of God and my knees were blackened and ashy from praying so long and hard. I tried new foods, like Couscous, listen to new music artist like Mumford and Sons and went on outdoor adventures like Zip-Lining. Before self-discovery, I would have never tried any of those things. Through self-discovery I realized that I loved speaking, working with children, hosting events and helping my community.

Despite not getting paid for it, I started doing more of what I loved to do and finding ways to make these activities a part of my everyday life. I learned that God will make room for my gifts if I am using them to honor his will for my life. (See Proverbs 18:16) I looked back on all my jobs and realized that I was chasing money, going for jobs that paid and offered more. I always managed to create another need that made me search for more and more money. Instead of a two-bedroom apartment, I "needed" a three-bedroom house. Instead of a local inexpensive beach getaway, I "needed" a butler-serviced all-inclusive Jamaican resort vacation. I bought kitchen appliances like a pasta maker and egg boiler that I never used when I could have just used a pot. The truth is the only thing I needed was to do what made me happy.

I'd like to propose a question to you, "How much passion do you have for the job you are in now?" I need you to have an honest conversation with yourself to determine if you are chasing money or chasing passion. Are you trusting God to make room for your gifts or working at the company that pays the most, but leaves you feeling empty? I get it, it's tough going to college, getting into a heap of student loan debt and coming out to find that there are no jobs in your field, so you take the highest paying offer you get. Most times this job has nothing to do with what you went to college for or what you love to do. I didn't want to work for Target coming out of college, but I had a daughter and bills to pay. After going from job to job, chasing the money for so long, I realized that no matter how much money I made it wasn't worth my happiness. Is what you're doing making you happy?

If you're a realist like me, then sometimes reality supersedes your faith. The reality is, if you don't work you don't eat. (See 2 Thessalonians 3:10) Sometimes, you might have to do what you have to do, suck it up, work the dead-end job, however, you must remember why you're doing it. When I first started hosting community events I had no sponsors and was using my personal funds to pay for everything. I became addicted to the pleasure and fulfillment I received from helping others that money was never a reason for me to stop. My paycheck from my full-time job allowed me to give back to the community the way I wanted too because I could afford it. The same goes for you, your "why" for working this job is to create some stability and resources for you to ultimately do what you love to do. However, don't get stuck in the resource, utilize the resource because your goal is to only do what you love. Here are some tips to help you dig deep within yourself to find your passion.

Dana Marie's 8 Tips for Positioning Passion

- **Take time to self-assess.**

   Ask yourself, "Am I doing what I love to do?" Take account of how you feel about your life and the things you currently do. How does being around children make you feel? Does cooking for others bring you pleasure? If you are doing what you love, then you're one lucky person. If not, then it's time for you to chase your passion. If you do what you love, you will always love what you do.

   "And do everything with love."
   1 Corinthians 16:14

- **Do some active soul searching**.

   Spend some time with yourself to learn who you truly are. Know your personality type, dreams, desires, and all that makes you who you are. You can meditate, pray, or go to a place of complete quiet. Make a list of all the things you currently enjoy doing, plan on doing and dream of doing. Prioritize what you love most and what you love the least. You'll be surprised at all the things you find most interesting. Pay more attention to the things that are at the top of your list because that is what will make you feel and live happier.

   "Do not neglect your gift, which was given you through prophecy when the body of elders laid their hands on you. Be diligent in these matters; give yourself wholly to them, so that everyone may see your progress."
   1 Timothy 4:14-15

- **Try new things; don't be afraid to discover all the facets of you.**

   It's perfectly okay that you might not even know what you love. I'll let you in on a secret, the more you experience the more you will learn about yourself. You won't know if you love swimming if you don't ever get in the water. You should make a goal to try as many new things as you can until you find something that brings you joyous fulfillment.

> *"Sow your seed in the morning, and at evening let your hands not be idle for you do not know which will succeed, whether this or that, or whether both will do equally well."*
> Ecclesiastes 11:6

- **Don't wait for anyone to validate your passion.**

   We often wait for people to give us permission to pursue our passion. If this is you, you'll never do what you love. You need to be proactive in pursuing your passion. If it makes you happy, then do it. People will tell you to wait until you have more money, wait until next year because it's too soon, but God didn't give them the burning desire you have. Just because they might not see the purpose in your passion, doesn't mean it's pointless. The only validation you need is God's.

   > *"Am I now trying to win the approval of human beings, or of God? Or am I trying to please people? If I were still trying to please people, I would not be a servant of Christ."*
   > Galatians 1:10

- **Remain steadfast in pursuing your passion.**

   You need to be so committed to doing what you love to do that nothing will stop you from doing it. Even if you work a full-time job, you still need to make time to do what you love. Make a commitment to yourself to always do you!

   > *"Therefore, my dear brothers and sisters, stand firm. Let nothing move you. Always give yourselves fully to the work of the Lord, because you know that your labor in the Lord is not in vain."*
   > 1 Corinthians 15:58

- **Continue to perfect your passion.**

    Practice, practice and guess what, practice. Don't ever get too content with your results because you will think there is never room for improvement. Find new ways to brush up on your skills as you develop an even deeper love for what you do.

    > *"Keep putting into practice all you learned and received from me--everything you heard from me and saw me doing. Then the God of peace will be with you."*
    > Philippians 4:9 NLT

- **Surround yourself with supportive people.**

    If you love doodling, but your family thinks it's stupid, then you might need to step back from them. No passion is too small and no passion is worthless. You must believe in your heart that what you love to do is the most amazing thing in the world and keep doing it. The people around should believe in you too.

    > *"Then I will give you shepherds after my own heart, who will lead you with knowledge and understanding."*
    > Jeremiah 3:15

- **Stay humble.**

    You might be in a position where your passion turns into profit; that's awesome. Always remember to stay humble despite your accomplishments. Don't forget about God and the people who supported you, having your back along the way. Allow room for growth and greater wisdom as God continues to lift you up.

    > *"Humble yourselves, therefore, under God's mighty hand, that he may lift you up in due time."*
    > 1 Peter 5:6

My goal is to get everyone in the world engulfed in his or her passion. People should be doing what they *love* to do on top of what they *must* do. If you make money doing what you love, that's a plus. But if you have to work a regular 9-5, at least come home and take the time out to do what you love. Your passion will lead you to your purpose; your purpose will lead to your profit. You just have to be ready to receive it!

CHAPTER FOURTEEN

WALKING IN YOUR PURPOSE

The most unanswered question in the world is, "What is my purpose?"

For a long time, I struggled finding this answer. Given all the jobs, experiences, and life lessons I still couldn't grasp the concept of having a purpose, knowing what it was and knowing how to execute it. I remember having breakdowns –like ugly cry, sniffling, falling out, slain on the floor type of breakdowns – because I felt useless. I thought that I was purposeless and not meant for anything. I didn't think that God would use me because of my past. I was molested as a kid, battling with major depression and was idolizing the men in my life. I struggled with making daily decisions to put God's desires over mine. I had more baggage than the airport. How could God have a purpose for little ole broken me?

I just knew for sure that I was going to roam the earth forever not understanding my purpose- one because I still didn't quite know what it was and secondly, I was ashamed of my past and thought God was too. You've probably noticed the pattern of my life now, I fell into deep crisis and then out of desperation, I ran back to God. That's exactly what I did. As I began to read the word especially about purpose, I noticed that God used broken people just like me to fulfill his divine purpose of bringing souls to Christ. Peter, one of Jesus's twelve disciples was a liar who ended up preaching/teaching the gospel of Jesus. Moses was a murderer who helped God's people in Egypt escaped the captive hand of Pharaoh and strengthen their faith in God. If God could forgive their sins, turn their lives around and use them to edify his purpose then why couldn't he use me, or better yet, use you! Discovering why you're here gives you a sense of worth and meaning, so I'm sure you can imagine how I felt when I didn't know my why. I would try to find my worth in every job I had, but I couldn't. I was so tired of living a miserable, and what seemed to be purposeless, life.

In January 2016, I started my strategic search aka New Year's resolution to find my divine purpose. I was single, fed-up and ready to embark on this mysterious journey. As I read scriptures like Psalms 139:13-14, the first things I noticed was that I had discovered my purpose a long time ago, but was too blind to see it. I realized that everything I was doing as a child and teen was connected to my purpose. At eight years old, I watched Oprah and said I wanted to be a television host. During middle school, I served as a volunteer for many community events because I liked serving others. I was an entertainer, dancer and amazing performer as a child. Ironically, at one point, when the pains of life overpowered purpose, I stopped doing everything I did as a child. I didn't perform, host, volunteer or serve my community. Emptiness plagued my heart, sorrow filled my spirit and I was disconnected from the will of God for my life.

When I reconnected to my purpose in 2016, I felt joy overtake my spirit and that emptiness in my heart was filled with love. Of course, I am continuously evolving, so my purpose will become more complex, however, I am still called to be a host, speaker, leader, teacher, helper, and server. As a child, we are introduced to things, whether dance class or science kits and through our free will we gravitate to the things that make us feel most happy and fulfilled. I found my purpose again when I backtrack to childhood. I had to dig deep to find out what made me most happy. I had to filter through my life experiences to find the purpose and connection to my destiny. For instance, I played the trumpet as a child, but being a musician wasn't a part of my purpose. I have no desire to play an instrument nor am I able to multitask on the level of a musician.

I remembered one of the old, gray-haired, stale candy hoarding church mother's saying to me, "Baaaabbbby, you are gonna be a star.

Your face is for TV and God is going to do it. Wait on it! Now give me some sugar."

I gladly received the affirmation, but the kisses were a little too much. However, the point is, she saw passion and purpose in me as a child. She watched how I spoke and touched the lives of other people at 8, so she imagined what I'd do at 28. She saw the greatness inside of me even as a child. It makes sense that your childhood passions would be connected to your purpose as well as your road of spiritual and self-discovery. I'm sure there's something you loved to do as a child that you might have left behind. Go back to reconnect with the passion because it could be tied to your purpose. As you read these tips on pursuing purpose remember that God, no matter how dark and ugly your past is, has a greater purpose for you, you just need to find it.

Dana Marie's 8 Tips for Pursuing Purpose

- **Tap back into your childhood and find that happy place.**

    Acknowledge the child that still lives within you because God most likely already showed you your purpose as a child. Remember what you used to do and how it made you feel. That's a part of who you are.

    > *"You made all the delicate, inner parts of my body and knit me together in my mother's womb."*
    > Psalms 139:13 NLT

- **Always live by your core values and beliefs.**

    The purpose God has for your life will directly correlate with what you believe. You must remain true to the positive moral values that were instilled in you during your development, whether in childhood or as an adult. Compromising your faith and belief in Jesus Christ isn't an option. Don't allow the world's perspective on life change what you know, according to the word of God, to be true.

    > *"Do not conform to the pattern of this world, but be transformed by the renewing of your mind. Then you will be able to test and approve what God's will is--his good, pleasing and perfect will."*
    > Romans 12:2

- **Develop a relationship with yourself.**

    This means that you spend more time with you. The more time you spend with yourself, exploring, learning, challenging and empowering you, the more you will uncover the real you. Without knowing who you are, and I mean without a best friend, a job title, a soul mate or even a dime to your name, you can't begin the search for your purpose. Fall in love with yourself, take care of yourself, enjoy yourself!

> *"After all, no one ever hated their own body, but they feed and care for their body, just as Christ does the church."*
> Ephesians 5:29

- **Set priorities in your life.**

Stop making time for things that aren't aligned with the vision you see for your life. Only do the things that bring you joy. Joy is more than happiness because happiness is contingent on what's happening when joy is always present whether things are happening or not. How you spend your time is how you spend your life. Do you really want to waste time on things that don't matter?

> *"Teach us to number our days, that we may gain a heart of wisdom."*
> Psalms 90:12

- **Find peace of mind.**

Pursuing your purpose will not be easy, but it will provide you with a sense of overwhelming peace, which ultimately leads to feeling joy. Some people are called to be janitors, while others are called to be motivational speakers for millions of people, but does that mean that one purpose is greater than the other. If you feel peace and contentment with the way your life is going, you are walking in purpose. God gives you free will to do whatever it is you want to do and if cleaning toilets give you peace, then I say do it and do it at 100%.

> *"The fruit of that righteousness will be peace; its effect will be quietness and confidence forever."*
> Isaiah 32:17

- **Make a difference in the world.**

    Although you can't save everybody, make a conscious effort to change what you can change. You can donate food/clothes to the homeless (See Luke 3:11), mentor a young teen (See Proverbs 22:6), provide financial support to a nonprofit organization serving the community (See Proverbs 19:16-17), whatever your heart desires to do, just make a difference. You should leave a legacy on earth as a servant, a helper and a change agent. As you begin to help/serve others they will begin to see the God and good in you.

    > *"In the same way, let your light shine before others, that they may see your good deeds and glorify your Father in heaven."*
    > Matthew 5:16

- **Seize the moment.**

    Your journey to finding purpose grows as you become more in tune with who you are and who you want to be. However, don't forget to enjoy the process. Live your life while you pursue purpose, hang out with like-minded individuals, take rejuvenating vacations, and spend time building your relationships with family and friends. Enjoy your life, while discovering your purpose.

    > *"The thief comes only to steal and kill and destroy; I have come that they may have life, and have it to the full."*
    > John 10:10

- **Understand that you have a shared purpose, especially with Christians.**

    Although you are individually extraordinary, don't allow your pride to stop you from connecting with other people to help ignite the shared purpose that you have. You are, great, talented, amazing, but sometimes your ego will destroy your ability to work together with people that have the same purpose as you. The more united you are with the body of Christ the more impact you will have on the world.

> *"For just as each of us has one body with many members, and these members do not all have the same function, so in Christ we, though many, form one body, and each member belongs to all the others."*
> Romans 12:4-5

Whatever your purpose is God has already put it inside of you. It's something that you won't necessarily need training for; it's a natural gift from God.

> *"We have different gifts, according to the grace given to each of us. If your gift is prophesying, then prophecy in accordance with your faith; if it is serving, then serve; if it is teaching, then teach; if it is to encourage, then give encouragement; if it is giving, then give generously; if it is to lead, do it diligently; if it is to show mercy, do it cheerfully."*
> Romans 12:6-8

Nestled inside you is a gift from God that he expects you to use to glorify his kingdom. Pay attention to the things that come naturally to you because they are most likely tied to your purpose. God wouldn't call you to be a singer and you can't hit one note with or without vocal lessons. On the contrary, your God-given gifts will qualify you for positions and experiences that you technically don't have the "so-called" training and experience for.

In all that you find you must also remember that your purpose is to be an ambassador for Christ. You were called to live a life like Jesus and spread the Gospel. You were called to praise God for all the things he's done, will do and won't do, for his "grace is sufficient for you". (See 2 Corinthians 12:9) You were called to show this carnal world that you could live a life of fun, love, joy, and peace while being a servant of God. If you never find your gift, but you're serving God and spreading the good news of Jesus Christ, you are already walking in your purpose!

CHAPTER FIFTEEN

BOSS LIVING = BOSS SACRIFICE

I truly believe that one achieves career freedom when they can choose what they do, when they do it, and with whom they do it. Often, I would get extremely bothered by the fact that I had someone dictating how I spent my time, when I ate my lunch and how many days I could get off to do things for myself. To make matters worse, I had someone controlling my every move and I didn't even like the job. Now I'm not writing this to discredit anyone with a regular 9-5 job, but the fact of the matter is when you are governed by someone who has the authority to dictate your schedule it can sometimes be daunting. These people have the power to tell you when to eat lunch, how long you take a break and even in most cases how many hours you can and cannot work. Where is the freedom in that?

As we remember what our goal in life is as Christians, to be more like Jesus, then we must realize that we have to be well-rounded individuals. He was a servant and a healer. A lover and a friend. A teacher and a leader, but he was also an entrepreneur. Like his earthly father Joseph, Jesus was a carpenter. (See Mark 6:3) He worked diligently with his hands to build quality furniture to sell to the people of Nazareth. Ultimately carpentry wasn't his divine purpose, but it gave him the resources he needed to fulfil what God needed him to do. God's divine purpose for Jesus was to save his people from eternal damnation and to show us how to live Godly lives in a secular world. Jesus taught us how to create a lifestyle where we are free to come, go and serve as we please. When Jesus was 30 years old we see him transition from carpentry to divinity, preaching and teaching the word of truth. We never heard anything about Jesus having a boss who told him that he can't go perform a miracle or preach the Gospel if he didn't have vacation time.

I want you to get to a point where you can freely determine how you spend your time, however, you must be smart. Like Jesus, don't quit your current job until you get the resources you need to excel on your entrepreneurial journey. If your current job can give you the startup money, increase your network and even provide training that relates to your business, stay there until you get what you need. Don't be a slacker or complainer because this isn't what you believe God called you to do, continue to work hard and as if you're doing it to glorify God, *"Whatever you do, work at it with all your heart, as working for the Lord, not for human masters."* (Colossians 3:23) However, remember not to get too comfortable; you have a goal to reach, a destiny to fulfil! Every step you take is a part of the strategic plan God has for your life. Your current job might be the very last job you have before you go into full-fledged entrepreneurship, so take all you can get.

Did you know that over 48% of Americans dream of being business owners? Out of that 48%, only about 15% actually make their dream a reality. My assumption is that the other 33% are either scared, unable to get the resources they need or just too darn lazy to put in the work to be their own boss. The interesting thing about most Americans, especially blacks, is we believe there is not enough room at the table for everyone to be a successful entrepreneur. I beg to differ. I believe that there is more than enough opportunity to create small businesses because there is always a need and desire for goods and services. As the population increases so will the need for childcare, food services, housing, recreation and new addictions like fidget spinners. So, take the notion that "there's not enough" and "everyone can't be an entrepreneur" out of your head!

Of course, there are major benefits to entrepreneurship, but despite the glamorous portrayal, there's a lot of sweat and blood put into the successfulness of any business. Too often people get caught up in the "hype" of entrepreneurship and forget to actually do the work. I see people wishing for someone else's business, but not willing to put in the sweat equity that they've put into their business to get it started, as well as, keep it running. It's more to just saying you're a business owner. You must eat sleep and breath it. A company like Walmart has employees working around the clock to make their business stay afloat, overnight crew, stockers, cashiers, greeters, sales, marketing and that's not even half of the team. In most cases, you won't even have a major team of employees at the beginning, so guess who's working day and night to run your business-- YOU!

Starting a business requires sacrifice. You will sacrifice your time, money, some relationships and whatever else gets in the way of making your dream a reality. During my journey of writing this book and starting a professional hosting business, Dana Speaks Life, LLC I realized that I was spending more time typing and researching local events than I was with my family. I couldn't go out for fun, unless it was a networking event because I had too many things to get done. The plan I had to travel the world flopped because my extra money went to my book and business. However, I established a healthy balance between the sacrifices I made and the ability to still enjoy the fruits of my labor. I scheduled family fun days, date nights and self-care time as well as business deadlines and networking opportunities. Did I always follow that plan? No! I had to alter my plan according to what or who needed my attention the most. Business, me or family.

My desire is that you take control of your own life and your own time. You can build your very own business and establish the flexibility you desire to do all the other things you want. No more asking to take a lunch break or to go to your family reunion. You can make your own decisions and call your own shots. You can live freely, despite all the sacrifices, you will make, which will ultimately be worth it. You can create a legacy and generational wealth for your children. Whether or not you already started your business these tips below will help you transition to the entrepreneur Jesus shows us how to be.

Dana Marie's 8 Tips for Building Bosses

- **Do your research and find your niche!**

    Before you jump right into your business do the background work. Answer these questions:

    a. "What should you sell? (Clothes, food, a service, etc.)

    b. Why should you sell it? (There's a need or want)

    c. Who should you sell it too? (Millennials, kids, families, etc.)

    d. Where should you sell it? (Local, national, etc.)

    e. How should you sell it? (Online, in-store)

    Remember creativity is key! Don't be scared to run with that crazy idea because someone, somewhere will buy it. Be sure to know your product and possess a deep understanding of the services you're providing before you sell them.

    > *"Desire without knowledge is not good,
    > how much more will hasty feet miss the way."*
    > Proverbs 19:2

- **Prioritize your business and create a work schedule.**

    Starting a business is very time-consuming. You must carve out time to do the things necessary to start and keep your business afloat. You most likely won't have someone holding you accountable to do what you need to do for your business, so you must make sure you do it yourself. Just like you would work a 9-5 and be there on time without missing days, you must do that same thing for your business. I strongly suggest hiring a business coach to help you stay focus if you know you struggle with accountability. Without a plan for your time, you will become busy doing nothing.

> *"We hear that some among you are idle and disruptive.*
> *They are not busy; they are busy bodies. Such people,*
> *we command and urge in the Lord Jesus Christ to*
> *settle down and earn the food they eat."*
> 2 Thessalonians 3:11-12

- **Set goals and celebrate your small successes.**

Every day/week you should make a list of goals you want to reach for your business. You should even go beyond that and list some action steps to reach the goals. Once you've checked off the goals on your list, celebrate yourself. Give yourself a pat on the back and words of encouragement. You've reached one of many goals you will accomplish throughout your entrepreneurial journey. Be proud of yourself.

> *"So do not throw away your confidence; it will*
> *be richly rewarded. You need to persevere so that*
> *when you have done the will of God, you will*
> *receive what he has promised."*
> Hebrews 10:35-36

- **Evaluate your progress.**

I can't stress enough how many business owners don't take the time out to assess their work ethic, product, revenue, and plan. You must determine if what you are doing is working as well as find new ways to improve and increase your business. Your small business is just the beginning, you can, if you desire, have a multimillion-dollar company. There are always ways to improve. As you seek wisdom and assess your current strategies you'll see that God will set you apart from those who don't pay attention to progress.

> *"I will do what you have asked. I will give you a wise and*
> *discerning heart, so that there will never have been anyone*
> *like you, nor will there ever be."*
> 1 Kings 3:12

- **Take time off!**

Wait, what...is probably what you're thinking. Yes. I just told you to work hard and stick to a schedule, but in your schedule, you need breaks. Although you want to be, you're not a machine. A break gives you the opportunity to reset, recharge and renew. You'll be surprised how many new and brilliant ideas you come up with when you take a moment to step away. Go on a mini vacation, the spa or just hang out in a good environment. Trust me, you need it more than you think, even God took a break on the seventh day!

> *"Six days do your work, but on the seventh day do not work, so that your ox and your donkey may rest, and so that the slave born in your household and the foreigner living among you may be refreshed."*
> Exodus 23:12

- **Build collaborative relationships.**

At some point during your entrepreneurial journey, you will realize that you have gone as far as you can go by yourself. Find opportunities for you to partner with organizations, businesses, and individuals that will best support your business. Be careful not to be a user. Before you ask for things, volunteer, donate and/or show genuine interest in your soon to be partner organization. The goal is to establish a relationship, not have a one-night stand. When you collaborate with someone, you work together, which means the task can get done sooner and better than expected.

> *"Two are better than one because they have a good return for their labor."*
> Ecclesiastes 4:9

- **Educate yourself and your team.**

There are tons of training classes, workshops, and events that you can attend to increase your skills and knowledge, as well as your success. Take advantage of the free educational opportunities first, which cut the cost of in-house training and development. When seeking paid training be sure that it's worth it. I don't care who's on the flyer, every event isn't worth your time and money. You can also hire a certified business coach to give you good advice and strategies on how to enhance your business.

> *"Let the wise listen and add to their learning,*
> *and let the discerning get guidance."*
> Proverbs 1:5

- **Enjoy the journey.**

I promise you that there will be good days and bad days during this journey of entrepreneurship. Learn to enjoy every moment. When it's good, celebrate, when it's bad, celebrate. Every step you take serves as a learning experience. You learn perseverance, patience, love, discernment, and diligence. Have fun with this because you are ultimately creating your own life. It would be wise for you to enjoy the process as you trust God every step of the way.

> *"Trust in the LORD with all your heart and lean not on*
> *your own understanding; in all your ways submit to him,*
> *and he will make your paths straight."*
> Proverbs 3:5-6

You have the power to change your life. You can't activate that power until you believe you have it. If every job you have has made you feel incomplete, lost and purposeless, then it's probably because you are not living the life God has planned for you to live. Don't be scared to start that catering business, sell those inspirational t-shirts or open your gym. You can do all things through Christ who strengthens you, so do it. There is more to your life than going to work 9-5 to make someone else rich, coming home, eating, sleeping and REPEAT. It's more inside of you and the only person that can bring it out is the Boss in you. Be *your* own boss, own *your* life and activate *your* power!

The Final Declaration

CHAPTER SIXTEEN

#NOLONGERBOUND

I truly hope that you've been inspired by my story. Despite having so many hardships in my life I realized that without them I wouldn't be the person I am now. My desire to help others, mentor young women and bring joy to the world would be null and void.

For so long, I couldn't make sense of everything that happened to me during my life, but now I see the purpose. My struggles make my successes even greater. Once I stop being the victim, my life started to change. I was freeing myself from the guilt, shame, doubt, carelessness, and heartbreak. My goal is to help people all over the world break the chains that are holding them back from living your best life.

Do you understand that you can live freely? You don't have to compromise with sorrow or barter with pain. You are victorious! Victors don't compromise and barter. They win by any means necessary. Take control of your spirit, finances, relationships, career, and mind. You possess the power to confidently live a life of freedom. God doesn't intend for you to be miserable during your one and only life. He wants more for you, but you have to take it. Take back your heart after it's been broken. Take back your mind after it's been tainted. Take back your finances after you've been poor for so long. The bondage that you're in will prevail no more. Say it with me, "The bondage I am in will prevail no more!"

Every area of your life has the potential of being the best area of your life. You can have joy all across the board. No settling! You can be spiritually healthy and still have financial freedom. You can have a "bomb" relationship and still be your own boss. You can even practice forgiveness and still have your sanity while doing it. It's all possible! How do I know--- because I'm doing it! My love life is great! In 2018, I'm marrying my best friend, the man of my dreams who shows me, agape love. Through constant prayer, bible study and surrounding myself with the amazing Christians at Epic Church, my faith is stronger. I'm walking in my purpose through my nonprofit organization, Focus Black Females, Inc where I empower, educate and enhance the community through workshops and events as well as conduct a mentoring program for young girls. This book alone is a gift from God that allows me to create a platform to share my story with other believers like you. I'm pregnant with possibilities and nothing will abort my dreams. I'm birthing greatness!

As you go through life, shaking loose the chains, use this book as a guide to help you when you get discouraged. When you feel lost, open the chapter that speaks to your situation. Ready to tackle your debt? Go to the "Slave to the Lender" chapter. Trying to set boundaries for your family? Go to "The Usual Family Drama" chapter. Most importantly open your bible, read it and meditate on it; hide his word in your heart so you can deal with life. Being a believer doesn't prevent you from going through difficult times, but it does give you tools and resources to get through them. (See John 16:33) Even Jesus went through trying times and we want to be like him, right?

I promise you, I am the happiest I've ever been because I follow everything I wrote in this book. I'm literally teaching you from experience. I didn't make this up. I lived it. I was so tired of living in captivity day after day. I knew the only way to gain freedom was to follow Jesus, activate my faith and trust in his word. I was angry with myself for not having the courage to take control of God's most precious gift to man – life. So, I took back my control in order to live the most abundant life God had planned for me. And guess what? God has a plan for your life too, but if you don't take the first step he won't make you. Like me, you will have moments when life seems too overwhelming, but remember you have the choice to live life free or in captivity. The decision is up to you!

THE VOW

THE VOW

On this day, _____, _____, 20_____, I, _____, have decided to LIVE LIFE FREE. I vow to commit to, with the help of God, freeing myself spiritually, mentally, relationally and financially. I will no longer be held in captivity, for I believe I have the power to live an abundant life, full of peace, joy, prosperity and longevity. Even when I have troubles, I will remain steadfast in faith, believing that I am a child of God who will reap all the promises in his holy word. I am no longer bound.

I will LIVE --- LIFE--- FREE!

_____

Sign

REFERENCES

"African American Retirement Insecurity." *Center for Global Policy Solutions*, globalpolicysolutions.org/resources/african-american-retirement-insecurity/.

"Black & African American Communities and Mental Health." *Mental Health America*, 3 Apr. 2017, www.mentalhealthamerica.net/african-american-mental-health.

ESV Study Bible: English Standard Version. Crossway Bibles, 2016.

Holmes, Tamara E. "Credit card race, age, gender statistics." *CreditCards.com*, Creditcards.com, www.creditcards.com/credit-card-news/race-age-gender-statistics.php.

Holy Bible: New Living Translation. Tyndale House Publishers, 2013.

"Household Debt Surpasses its Peak Reached During the Recession in 2008." *Household Debt Surpasses its Peak Reached During the Recession in 2008 - FEDERAL RESERVE BANK of NEW YORK*, www.newyorkfed.org/newsevents/news/research/2017/rp170517.

"Marriage in Black America." *BlackDemographics.com*, blackdemographics.com/households/marriage-in-black-america/.

"NAMI." *African Americans | NAMI: National Alliance on Mental Illness*, www.nami.org/Find-Support/Diverse-Communities/African-Americans.

Holy Bible: the new King James version, containing the Old and New Testaments. Thomas Nelson Bibles, 1982.

Syswerda, Jean. *NIV women of faith study bible: New International Version*. Zondervan, 2001.

The Open Bible New American Standard Version. Thomas Nelson Inc, 2004.

NOTES

NOTES

NOTES

www.ingramcontent.com/pod-product-compliance
Lightning Source LLC
Chambersburg PA
CBHW051105160426
43193CB00010B/1322